WHAT CHRISTIANS
BELIEVE

D.229

Elizabeth Anne Burt

WHAT CHRISTIANS BELIEVE

John Eddison

HODDER AND STOUGHTON
LONDON SYDNEY AUCKLAND TORONTO

British Library Cataloguing in Publication Data

Eddison, John
   What Christians Believe
   1. Theology, Doctrinal
   I. Title
   230   BT77.3

ISBN 0 340 26361 X

CONTENTS

1   God

Christians are not the only people who believe in God. In fact, whenever a poll is taken as to whether people believe or not, there is nearly always a majority who think that some sort of supreme being or power lies behind the universe.

Roughly speaking, those who answer 'Yes' to this question divide into one or other of two main classes, or veer towards one of two poles. There are first of all the 'pantheists' who regard God as some kind of life-force, permeating His creation, and indistinguishable from it; while on the other hand there are the 'deists' who think of Him as being completely separate from the universe, divorced from it in any personal sense, and simply the being who set it all going in the first place, and then, so to speak, retired from the scene. Pantheists identify God with nature, while deists isolate Him from it.

It would be a considerable over-simplification to say that Pantheism is the religion of the far east, and Deism of the west, but in so far as these two hemispheres are represented by Hinduism and Islam respectively, there is perhaps some truth in the claim.

Christians, like Jews, refuse to go to either extreme. To them God is distinct from His creation, and yet involved with it; He is outside it, and yet intimately concerned with it; transcendent and at the same time immanent. And it is this fact which leads us at once to the first attribute which we find ascribed to Him in the Bible: He is *personal*.

We have to be careful when we use this word. It would be quite wrong to suppose that God is simply some sort of super-person, 'man writ large'. What we mean by the word is that He is capable of entering into personal dealings with His creatures, and of communicating to them His will and purpose, and enabling them to converse with Him.

We might take a useful analogy from the relationship which exists between a man and his dog. If for a moment, and for the purpose of this argument, we credit the dog with the power of human reasoning, it might argue in this manner: 'There is an area where the ec-centric circles of our lives, my master's and mine, overlap. He feeds me, walks me, pets me, and in this area where we communicate, and which involves loyalty and obedience on my part and loving concern on his, it is reasonable for me to speak of him as "canine".

'On the other hand, there are large areas of his activity and existence which are completely beyond my ken. I have no idea what he is up to when he sets off in his car each morning, or takes a book from his shelves in the evening. He inhabits a world at whose nature I can only guess, and it is far beyond my capacity to understand what it is all about.'

Of course, like all analogies, this one breaks down. It does so when we remember that the man is equally mystified by some of the habits and activities of his dog, whereas in the case of God we believe that there is not a thought in our minds which He does not understand, and that nothing we do or suffer will take us beyond the reach of His sympathy and love.

But as far as it goes it is helpful, because it serves to show that although there is communication between God and man, and He is intimately concerned with our welfare, yet this fact by no means exhausts the limits of His divine nature. God does not exist for our benefit, any more than the man can be said to exist for the benefit of the dog. There is much about God which it is within man's grasp to understand, appreciate and enjoy; but there is infinitely more which is far beyond our understanding, and the child's question, 'What does God do all day?' remains unanswered and unanswerable.

Majestic mystery shrouds those mountain peaks
Of whose green foothills man with knowledge speaks.

But in what particular ways do Christians believe that God deals with them personally? What corresponds in man's experience to what the dog might describe as 'the canine attributes' of its owner? First of all, he looks upon God as the *Creator*. The universe, he argues, cannot have come about through the purely fortuitous conjunction of atoms, and if there were nothing in the first place, there would be nothing now. In his view it is the product of purposeful action on the part of a wise and all-powerful creator, and bears every mark of intelligent design. The psalmist realized this when he said, 'the heavens proclaim the glory of God, and the firmament reveals His handiwork' (Psa. 19.1).

A hundred years ago a great battle raged between the disciples of Charles Darwin, with their theories of evolution, and Christians, who held to a literal interpretation of the opening chapters of Genesis. It is doubtful whether today the opposing lines are quite so sharply drawn up, and many Christians see nothing that detracts from 'the glory of God' or the wonders of His 'handiwork' in some theories of creative evolution which allow room in their process for the special place occupied by man, and his unique relationship with his Maker.

It is because He is our Maker that God's relationship with us is so different from the one we considered between the man and his dog; for in no sense can man be regarded as a creator, even of his own children. God, having in His power and wisdom created us, understands us completely, and the psalmist (Psa. 139) pictures Him working to a sort of 'blue-print' in making us. It follows, therefore, that we can only fulfil His purpose for us, and function properly, if we allow ourselves to be 'serviced' and 'maintained' by Him.

But the Bible goes further than this, for it presents God to us not only as a Maker, but as *Father*. We have to treat this word carefully, because it would be more precise to say that He is 'father-like' or 'paternal'; for we are created by God, and not begotten. Christians believe that Jesus is the 'only begotten Son of God' (John 3.16), and that it is only in and through Him that we are accepted as children into God's family (Gal. 3.26).

Although therefore we cannot strictly speaking say that all men are the sons of God, the metaphor reminds us that in His relation to His creatures, God exhibits all those qualities which we associate with fatherhood (Psa. 103.13). Indeed, Paul would not allow us to use the word 'metaphor' at all, because he maintains that all fatherhood is derived from God. His is the original, and human fatherhood only a copy. In other words, in attributing fatherhood to God we are not suggesting that He is behaving like us, but rather that human fatherhood is our attempt to behave like Him (Eph. 3.14, 15).

Nowadays it is regrettably true that the word 'Father' does not always call to mind those qualities which were once, and always should be, associated with it. But the good father is surely recognized by one thing supremely, namely his love. (The New Testament uses the word *philoteknos* – Tit. 2.4 – to describe this sort of love, as distinct from *philodelphia*, or 'brotherly love'.)

Besides natural affection, perhaps the most distinctive feature of such paternal love is that it desires and seeks the very highest and best for its object. It aims, not just to make the loved one happy, but also good, and this means that it has about it an element of discipline, and provides a moral framework within which the child can grow from the security of infancy to the liberty of manhood (Heb. 12.5–11).

And that is the way in which God loves us. There is nothing sentimental or permissive about His love. He sets the very highest standards, and demands the best, because it is His purpose to reproduce within us the likeness of His only begotten Son, Jesus Christ.

There is a third picture of God which emerges from the Bible – that of *Judge* or *King*. He is presented to us as the moral governor of the universe. It is sometimes argued that this cannot be so, that God has lost control of His universe, and that we are living in a runaway world. But we must remember that there are only two ways in which He could have made us: as robots or automata, incapable of independent action; or as free agents with the capacity to choose their own way if they felt like it, rather than His. In granting man freewill, and, so to speak, 'dominion status', He ran the risk that we would declare 'unilateral independence'; and of course that is precisely what we have done.

But we are frequently reminded in the Bible that against all appearances, God has not lost control, that all things will ultimately be subjected to His authority (1 Cor. 15.24–28; Heb. 2.8, 9), and that the day will come when 'the kingdoms of this world will become the kingdoms of our Lord, and of His Christ; and He shall reign for ever and ever' (Rev. 11.15). However fiercely the world may fight against God and resist His sovereignty, it cannot break from His control. In the end it will have to submit, and, as the psalmist reminds us, the last laugh is His (Psa. 2.2–4).

In June 1940, after the fall of France, the Germans had a saying, 'The war is won, but it's not yet over.' How wrong they were, we now know, but the Christian may fairly apply those words to the world-situation as it is today. The war has been won. The power of evil has been broken. The enemy is mortally wounded. It is true that we do not yet see all things subdued to God, for 'V-Day' is still in the future. The King has acceded, but He has yet to be crowned.

It is in these three senses, therefore, that the Christian speaks of God as being 'personal'. He reveals Himself to us as Creator, Father and King. He made us, He loves us, and He will finally reign over us. But as we have considered all this, another important aspect of His nature has begun to emerge, namely that He is also a *moral* being.

From the start to the finish of the Bible this fact stands out with startling clarity. The first picture we have of man's relationship with God is in a garden, from which, because of his disobedience, he is expelled, and forbidden to re-enter. And when we turn from the opening chapters of Genesis to the closing chapters of Revelation, the picture is the same, except that this time, instead of a garden, we have a city; and rather in the same way as we find a notice at the entrance to a motorway forbidding access to certain kinds of driver and vehicle, so over the gates of the celestial city we find this warning: 'Nothing unclean shall enter it, nor anyone who practises abomination or falsehood' (Rev. 21.27).

And all the way between these two extremes, from the garden to the city, the picture we are given of God is the same. It is of someone who is unutterably holy, too holy to have any form of communication with man who, we are told, 'drinks iniquity like water' (Job 15.16). An 'iron curtain' has descended between man and God, breaking the fellowship we were created to enjoy (Isa. 59.1, 2).

The Bible uses three principal ways of bringing home to man the holiness of God. First, there is the standard set in the Ten Commandments and the teaching of Moses. Paul tells us that one of the purposes of the Commandments was that 'sin . . . might be shown to be sin' (Rom. 7.13); in other words, that it might be recognized for what it really is, an offence against God. Has someone ever said to you, 'I am afraid you would be breaking the law', when you have been thinking of doing something which you may have known to be wrong, but you thought was perfectly legal? In the same way the Ten Commandments reveal the really serious nature of sin by showing us that it is the breaking of God's Law.

And it was because of man's lawlessness that there had to be introduced the whole vast apparatus of ceremony and sacrifice which was designed to show that God could only be approached by those who have 'clean hands and a pure heart' (Psa. 24.4). Just as a certain protocol and ritual have to be observed before an ordinary citizen can have an audience of the Queen, so the elaborate system of animal sacrifices taught man that, because of his sin, the God to whom he wanted to be presented must first be propitiated.

In the second place the same theme was taken up by the prophets in their challenge. 'Which of us can dwell with everlasting fire?' asked the prophet Isaiah (Isa. 33.14). In the early days of space travel, the problem which most worried the astronauts was that of re-entry into the earth's atmosphere. If the angle was too shallow, they would bounce off into an everlasting orbit; while if on the other hand it was too sharp, then they would be burnt to a cinder. It had to be just right. So it is that the psalmist asks, 'Who shall ascend into the hill of the Lord, or who shall dwell in His holy place?' (Psa. 24.3). The answer is, only those whose hearts and hands have been cleansed from sin; only the humble and contrite can dwell with Him 'whose name is holy' (Isa. 57.15).

Finally and fully, this majestic holiness of God is portrayed for us in the life and example of Jesus Himself. The fact that He Himself forgave people their sins (Mark 2.5–10), and taught them to ask for forgiveness (Luke 11.4), and yet never did so Himself would suggest in ordinary people a fairly advanced degree of insanity. But that is not our reaction in the case of Jesus, because we find that no one was able to accuse Him of sin (John 8.46). His enemies could find no fault with Him (Matt. 27.4; Luke 23.4); those whom we might describe as neutral said the same (Luke 23.41, 47); while His friends were unanimous in their verdict: 'He did no sin,' said Peter (1 Pet. 2.22). 'He knew no sin,' added Paul (2 Cor. 5.21). While John who perhaps had an even deeper insight, and knew Him better than anyone, declared, 'In Him is no sin' (1 John 3.5).

And so in these three familiar ways, by precept, by persuasion and by picture, the tremendous truth of God's holiness was brought home to man, and we are taught that the one with whom we have to do is of 'purer eyes than to look upon evil' (Hab. 1.13). If therefore there is to be any communication between man and such a God, it can only be on a moral basis, that is to say, after the question of sin has been settled and dealt with.

Continuing the Bible picture of God, we see, next that He is a *spiritual* being. This means that He is someone whose existence does not depend upon a physical body, even though at times He may choose to use one in order to manifest Himself in a special way.

'God is spirit' (John 4.24), we are told, and the word 'spirit' is closely related, in both Hebrew and Greek to 'breath' or 'wind'. We shall return to this theme in a later chapter, when we come to think about the Holy Spirit, but for the present it is worth noting what is implied in this comparison between spirit and wind.

First of all, both are universal. Wherever we go we find the wind. We meet it in the Arctic snow-storm, the Atlantic gale, or the sand-storms in the deserts of North Africa. It is inescapable. In the same way we cannot escape the presence of God. The psalmist explored this possibility, and wrote of his experience as follows: 'Where can I escape from Thy Spirit? Where can I flee from Thy presence? If I climb up into heaven, Thou art there: if I make my bed in hell, again I find Thee. If I take the wings of the morning, and dwell in the uttermost parts of the sea; even there Thy hand shall lead me, and Thy right hand shall hold me' (Psa. 139.7–10).

But at the same time, the wind is local and individual. You can have it, so to speak, 'all to yourself', and in a sailing boat at sea, or on an exposed headland, or walking over a moor, the wind seems to belong to you in a personal and individual way.

There is a book with the title *London Belongs to Me*, and there is a sense, of course, in which that is nonsense. London belongs to no one, or perhaps to everyone. But we can see just what it means. Each of us as individuals may enjoy the sights and sounds of London, visit it, stay there and live there if we want to. We become 'Londoners'. London belongs to us, just as we belong to it. And so it is with God. We read that Enoch 'walked with God' (Gen. 5.22) and that Moses 'talked with Him' (Ex. 33.9); and in experiences like those, they, and millions like them, could truthfully say of this great, universal Being, whom 'heaven itself, the highest heaven cannot contain' (1 Kings 8.27), 'He belongs to me.'

And so we come to the fourth and final attribute of God which we must consider, and that is that He is an *eternal* being. It would be a mistake to confine the meaning of this word simply to 'everlastingness'. No doubt it includes that idea, but also very much more. It means that God is boundless, and outside our world, much in the same way as the man is outside the world of his dog, or the author is outside his play or book.

It is for this reason that the human mind breaks down or 'cuts out' when we try to think of eternity, or what the prophet meant when he said that God 'inhabits eternity' (Isa. 57.15); and though theologians, philosophers and poets have done their best, it remains a concept which we have not the necessary apparatus to understand with our limited, finite minds.

When thinking of God as a spiritual being, we noticed His complete independence of matter. To describe Him as eternal is a way of saying that He is also totally independent of time and space. 'One day with the Lord is like a thousand years, and a thousand years like one day' (2 Pet. 3.8). In other words, God is outside our system of reckoning time altogether. With Him there is, so to speak, no past or present, but an everlasting 'now'.

If we go back to the analogy of the relationship existing between the author and his book, we can see how he and his characters move in a different time-sequence. For example, events which may actually take a hundred years to happen can be telescoped into five minutes' reading; while he may spend hours depicting a scene which in fact only lasts for a few minutes. 'One day' with the author could be 'a thousand years' for his characters, and vice versa.

This 'nowness' of God was well illustrated by C. S. Lewis

when discussing the subject of prayer, and considering how
God can deal with the millions of requests which must land
upon His desk at the same moment. He said that God had
all eternity to answer the split-second prayer of an airman
who was being shot down in flames. It is rather like the
experience we have with a moving object. The further away
we are from it, the slower its movement seems to be, and if
we could reach a theoretically infinitely distant point and
still see the object, it would appear to be stationary.

If therefore we represent time by a straight line, produced
indefinitely, eternity is represented, not by a continuation
of that line into the infinite distance, but by a circle moving
at right angles to it, or even spiralling along its length.
Perhaps this was in the mind of Henry Vaughan in his
'Silex Scintillanus', where he sees time as a kind of shadow
of eternity.

> I saw eternity the other night,
> Like a great ring of pure and endless light,
>   All calm as it was bright;
> And round beneath it, time in hours, days, years,
>   Driven by the spheres
> Like a vast shadow mov'd; in which the world
>   And all her train were hurl'd.

It won't have escaped the reader that the God we have
described so far is a God that fits other religions as well as
Christianity. True, we have employed some supporting
evidence from the New Testament, but there is little or
nothing which has been said about Him so far with which a
believing Jew would disagree. His God too is personal,
moral, spiritual and eternal. In what way then is the
Christian's God unique?

It is in the claim that He has revealed Himself to us, not
just in the ancient ritual and ceremony, or in the teaching
of the prophets, nor even in those rare but vivid theophanies,
but in the person of His Son, Jesus Christ. Nowhere is this
truth more beautifully or completely expressed than in the
Epistle to the Hebrews which was written, we must remember, to devout Jews, to help them to reach a fuller understanding of the God whom they worshipped. 'God, who at
sundry times and in divers manners spoke in time past to

the fathers by the prophets, has in these last days spoken to us by His Son . . . being the brightness of His glory and the express image of His person' (Heb. 1.1–3).

In other words, the writer is telling us that the Old Testament picture of God is not complete. It is not God's 'last word'. The final, perfect picture was presented to us in the person of our Lord Jesus Christ. As people studied His life, they found that it endorsed everything they had been taught about God, but it did so in a way which they could appreciate with their physical senses. They saw living among them the physical embodiment of absolute holiness, almighty power, infinite wisdom and boundless love.

'God is light' (1 John 1.5), we are told. But light is invisible. It is not an object of sight, but a medium of sight: not something we look at, but through. If you want to see light, you have to pass it through a prism, and break it up into the constituent colours of the spectrum. That is what Jesus did for us, and in this way the God whom no man has seen at any time, 'immortal, invisible', is displayed before us in human form in the person of His Son.

Finally, what should be our reaction to this God? The Old Testament makes frequent use of the word 'fear'. At first sight it suggests an unsatisfactory, defensive and even negative attitude to adopt towards such a wonderful being; but rightly understood the word embraces every mood which the thought of God should inspire in the human heart, from outright terror to adoring love.

I remember how this was brought home to me once when a boy asked me what it meant to 'fear God'. We were standing near the sea at the time, and pointing towards it I said, 'It is like that. I love the sea. I like to be in it, beside it and on it. But I have a tremendous respect, even reverence for it. I know something of its awe-ful majesty and power, and I would never take liberties with it.' That is what it means to 'fear God'. And if you think about it, that same sort of mixed emotional reaction is what we experience when we are faced with any of the great elemental forces of nature – wind, fire, thunder, water and so on; and is it not therefore appropriate that we should feel the same towards their Maker?

> Oh how I fear Thee living God,
>   With deepest, tenderest fears;

And worship Thee with trembling hope
  And penitential tears.
Yet I may love Thee too, O Lord,
  Almighty as Thou art;
For Thou has stooped to ask of me
  The love of my poor heart.

2   Jesus Christ

'Born in an obscure village, in a remote corner of the Roman Empire, and cared for by humble, working-class parents, he never went to a university, never travelled beyond the borders of his own country, never married or took up a professional or political career. He had no settled home, made no money, led no army, wrote no book, left no legacy, and at the time of his death was unknown outside the country of his birth. Finally, at an age when most men are reaching responsible levels in the career of their choice, he was framed by the authorities, betrayed by a colleague, deserted by his friends, and, after a mock trial, was executed for treason.

'And yet today, nearly two thousand years later, this man is followed, loved and worshipped by millions of people who have never seen him, but to whom he is a hero, a deliverer and a God. Thousands have regarded him as dearer than life itself, and have gladly accepted imprisonment and death rather than abandon their allegiance to him; while countless others have made service to him and his cause the chief purpose of their existence. Never in the history of the human race has one man meant so much to so many.'

There can be very few people, whether Christians or not, who would quarrel with that assessment of Jesus of Nazareth; and it is that phenomenon which it is the purpose of this chapter to examine, and if possible to explain.

Who was He? The superficial answer is obvious. He was the eldest son of Mary, a Hebrew girl engaged to be married to a man named Joseph, who traced his descent back to David and beyond. But there was clearly a mystery surrounding the circumstances of His birth, the more critical and cynical believing that Joseph had adopted a baby born to Mary by some other man, and out of wedlock.

But this was certainly not what Mary herself or Joseph believed. Their accounts, supplied to Luke and Matthew, attributed the birth of Jesus to the operation of the Holy

Spirit who made the part usually played by a father un-
necessary. In other words, and as the Apostles' Creed puts it,
Jesus was 'conceived by the Holy Ghost, born of the Virgin
Mary'.

As the baby grew up into boyhood and manhood, this
explanation of His birth, quite apart from any Old Testament prophecies and the claims of His parents, began to look
more and more reasonable. Every stage of His life was
attended by miraculous events, and it was therefore logical
to assume that His birth too was out of the ordinary. Would
not the opposite have been surprising? Was it not to be
expected that someone who had healed the sick and raised
the dead, and who Himself had returned from the grave and
then left the earth in a miraculous manner should have
entered the world in an extraordinary and unusual way?

Furthermore, there were the claims which He made for
Himself – claims which were eventually to form the basis
of the charges levelled against Him. He began by announc-
ing His authority to forgive sins (Mark 2.5), thus apparently
usurping the prerogative of God Himself; and He ended by
claiming equality with God – to have come from Him and
to be returning to Him again (John 5.18).

In anyone else such claims would have sounded pre-
posterous. They would have been exposed as fraudulent, and
the person making them would have been certified as insane.
But somehow we do not find ourselves reaching that sort of
conclusion about Jesus. The claims rang true. They were
consistent with the rest of His teaching. They were endorsed
by His followers and confirmed by His miracles. They were
all of a piece, and slowly His disciples were driven to the
conclusion that their Master was the denizen of a different
world from theirs. It was only logical therefore to believe
that His arrival in this world should be in keeping with the
way in which the rest of His life was lived, and it no longer
seemed strange or unreasonable to think of Him as 'conceived by the Holy Ghost, born of the Virgin Mary'.

And not only logical, but theological; for if Jesus was
what He claimed to be, the Son of God, the 'God-Man', was
it not necessary for His birth to be both natural and supernatural? How else would we have expected such a person to
enter the world? If He had come in the normal way, there
would have been no distinctive mark of divinity upon Him;

and if He had come, let us say, straight from heaven in a chariot of fire, He would never have been properly human. He came in the only possible way which was open to Him.

It is as the God-Man that Christians think of Jesus Christ, but it is a phrase which needs careful definition. It suggests a sort of hybrid, like the legendary Centaur, half man and half horse. But that is not what we believe about Jesus. He was perfect and complete man and at the same time perfect and complete God.

Perhaps this illustration will help. There is nothing in its appearance which immediately distinguishes a 'live rail' from its fellows. The colour and texture are the same. And yet we know that it is permeated with a power which the others do not possess, and that when we say simply that it is 'an iron rail' we have not said the most important thing about it.

So there may have been very little to distinguish Jesus from His fellow men. We have no contemporary picture or description to guide us. We like to think of Him as being tall and handsome, but the traditions are vague and misleading. We know that physically He was like other men, and could experience hunger, thirst and tiredness, and that He could suffer pain. Emotionally too, He knew the meaning of sorrow and joy, and He could feel compassion, sympathy and anger. In fact there is nothing that we know about Him to suggest that He was not completely human, and yet running right through that humanity was the current of His divine nature. He differed from other men not in degree, but in kind. It was not just that He was braver, wiser, humbler, kinder than they, but He belonged to a different order. He was related to God in a different, a unique way, as we saw in the last chapter; ordinary men are created by God, but Jesus was begotten; ordinary men are God's creatures, but Jesus was His Son (Heb. 1.5, 6).

It has fairly been argued that if Jesus was not God, then He was either mad or bad: 'aut Deus, aut homo non bonus'. The one thing we cannot call Him is 'a good man'. Either He was very much more, or He was very much less; for in making the claims He did make, He must either have been crazy or else perpetrating a most deliberate fraud. Either we have to admit that He was God, or we can choose between calling Him a crank or a crook.

William Hazlitt, in one of his essays, tells the well-known story about the dinner party which Charles Lamb gave for some of his friends. The conversation turned to some of the famous figures of history whom they would like to meet, and someone mentioned the name of Jesus Christ. There was silence for a moment, and then Charles Lamb said in his slow, gentle, stammering way, 'If Shakespeare came into the room, we would all stand up; but if He came in, we would fall on our faces before Him.' No one less than God Himself would evoke that kind of spontaneous reaction on the part of men and women.

But it was only slowly that this tremendous truth dawned upon the minds of the disciples while Jesus was with them. There were moments of rare insight, as for example when Simon Peter made his famous declaration – 'Thou art the Christ, the Son of the living God' (Matt. 16.13–17); but these would be followed by periods of obtuseness when 'their eyes were holden' (Luke 24.13–29). It was left to the Holy Spirit to bring the light fully into their minds, and to turn the puzzle into a picture (John 16.12–15).

Thus it is only in the later books of the New Testament (although we must remember that they were actually written before the gospels) that the writers began to formulate what is meant by the 'incarnation'. 'In Him [that is Jesus]', says Paul, 'dwells all the fullness of the Godhead in bodily form' (Col. 2.9); for 'great is the mystery of our religion: God manifest in the flesh' (1 Tim. 3.16). While the writer to the Hebrews describes Jesus as 'the brightness of God's glory', bearing 'the very stamp of His nature' (Heb. 1.3).

The exact nature of what is called 'the hypostatic union', that is to say, the relationship within the person of Christ of His Godhead to His Manhood, was a matter of considerable debate for several centuries after His coming. In AD 451 at the Council of Chalcedon there was issued what was known as the 'Definition' which has guided the Christian Church ever since.

In effect it defined the person of Christ in negative terms. It opposed those who sought to make 'a mixture or a compound' of the two natures, human and divine; and also those who tried to explain it by the co-existence of 'a pair of sons'. Put positively, it was claimed that the Scriptures taught that 'the property of each nature is preserved and concurs in one Person'. This means that when we speak of the 'God-Man', we do not mean two separate persons, nor do we imply an amalgam of two natures; but rather one person with two natures, human and divine, existing together in perfect harmony.

We must now ask a second question. If Jesus really was what He claimed to be, namely the Son of God, *Why did He come?* That is a question that would make nonsense in any entry in 'Who's Who'. That book is concerned with what people have done, their achievements and activities. The question of motive does not arise.

But the question, 'Why were you born?' so meaningless if put to ordinary people applies most pertinently to Christ. If He was indeed the Son of God, then His birth was no accident, nor did it depend upon the will of man, but was His chosen method of entry into the world. He might have come in some other way, or He might not have come at all. Why then did He come?

Before going on to try to answer that question, it is worth considering the circumstances of His birth – the people He came to, the place and the time chosen.

For centuries God had been preparing one nation, which had grown from a tribe, a family and an individual, to be the 'cradle' for the Messiah, 'the desire of all nations' (Hag. 2.7). He might have chosen any race for this purpose, but the fact that He chose the Jews explains why it was to them that Jesus came in the first instance.

And we can see the divine wisdom in this choice when we remember the astonishing gift which the Jews possess for dissemination. In almost every country in the world they have adapted and applied themselves. For centuries, until the State of Israel was created after the Second World War they had no national home of their own, and even today we rarely apply the single word 'Jew' to anyone. They are always 'German Jews', 'Polish Jews', 'British Jews', and so on, which in itself is a testimony to their singular capacity to become absorbed into the country of their adoption, and yet to retain their essential identity.

We see the beginning of this in New Testament days, for in Asia Minor and Italy it was always to the Jewish community that Paul turned first, because they constituted the natural depository for the gospel, and the vehicle for its transmission to other countries. Perhaps more often than they realize, and in spite of their opposition to Christianity, the Jews have been the unconscious 'carriers' of the gospel to other lands.

It has often been pointed out too, that by coming as He did to Israel, Jesus chose the place which at that time and ever since has been the strategic centre, the fulcrum of the world – the place where three continents, Asia, Africa and Europe converge. Nowhere, certainly in the ancient world, could you have planted a message in the hope that it would spread more quickly.

So much for the people and the place, but consider also the time that was chosen, what Paul called 'the right time' (Gal. 4.4). For the spread of any message two things are necessary, a common language and a satisfactory system of communication, and these were provided by the Greeks and the Romans. Greek was virtually the *lingua franca* of those days, and would get you anywhere; while the Roman passion for building roads provided ready made routes for missionaries to follow.

In other words, if God had something to say to His creation, and wanted to spread the message as widely and as quickly as possible, the circumstances could hardly have been more favourable.

But we must return to our question: Why did Jesus come? What had God to say through Him which was so special? The purpose of Jesus' coming may be summed up in one sentence: He came to do the will of God (John 5.30; 6.38), wherever it might lead Him and whatever it might cost. From His first recorded words ('Do you not know that I must be about My Father's business?' – Luke 2.49) to His last recorded prayer ('Not My will, but Thine be done' – Luke 22.42) this was His one aim and ambition, the thread that ran right through His life from start to finish, and on which all the events, like beads, were hung. The will of God was the one thing that mattered beyond any other to Jesus. It was His business or work, His food (John 4.34) and His recreation (Psa. 40.8); whilst the society He enjoyed most was to be found amongst those who shared His outlook in this matter (Mark 3.35). We often say of someone, 'I wish I knew what made him tick'. What made Jesus 'tick' was obedience to the will of God. That was the mainspring of

His life, or the main line along which He travelled.

But in what way was that aim to be achieved? What was the will of God for Jesus? Where did it lead Him? Why did He have to come? The incarnation had two main results. First, Jesus revealed God to man. There was of course much about God that had already been revealed in nature, history and experience, but the picture was still incomplete. Philip's request, 'Show us the Father, and we shall be satisfied' (John 14.9) was a very natural and a very human one, and it echoed the longing in many hearts. What was God like – the 'God whom no man has seen or can see' (1 Tim. 6.16)? We may learn a great deal about a man from his garden, his library, his letters and his friends, but until we have the chance to meet him face to face, our knowledge is at best sketchy and second-hand. We are rather like the Queen of Sheba, when she was first introduced to the glory of Solomon, 'She said to the king, "The report was true which I heard in my own land of your affairs and of your wisdom, but I did not believe the reports until I came and my own eyes had seen it; and behold, the half was not told me; your wisdom and prosperity surpass the report which I heard" ' (1 Kings 10.6, 7).

And so on that first Christmas Day the ancient cry – 'Will God indeed dwell on the earth?' (1 Kings 8.27) was answered by the birth of Jesus, one of whose names was 'Emmanuel', which means 'God with us' (Matt. 1.23). In other words, in Jesus Christ we have a bodily manifestation of the nature and character of God (Col. 2.9). It is not that we see all of God there is to know, for that would be impossible to finite minds; but we see all of God that can be expressed in human terms.

We can imagine how some composer might transcribe a symphony so that it could be performed upon a piano. Obviously there would be limitations to the process, because for one thing the notes of the piano could not be a complete substitute for the instruments of the orchestra. The composer is trying, so to speak, to express in two dimensions what really requires three; but the translation is perfectly authentic and as complete as the piano will allow. So it was that in Jesus Christ God translated Himself into human terms, making the immortal, invisible God audible, tangible and visible (1 John 1.1–3).

In the Sistine Chapel in Rome there is a painting by Guido Reni called 'Dawn'. But because it is painted upon a very high ceiling it is difficult for those standing below to appreciate it properly. Immediately beneath it, therefore, there has been placed a table with a highly polished mirror as its surface, so that what exists above may be enjoyed and experienced below, and revealed to viewers in all its detail.

And what did Jesus reveal to us of the character of God? All those things that we considered in the last chapter. In the sinless life of Jesus we see the holiness of God; in His miracles, the power of God; in His teaching, the wisdom of God; and in His death and passion, the love of God. It was as though a great playwright deserted for a time the warmth and comfort of his library, and came on to the stage to take the part of one of his own characters. For the first time people had the chance to see the perfect interpretation of the author's own mind.

But if it had not been for man's fall from grace, through his own disobedience, he would never have lost his original vision of God, and therefore needed this special revelation; and so this reason for the coming of Christ is only subsidiary to its main purpose, which was to redeem man to God.

The whole New Testament bears witness to this fact. It was as a 'Saviour' that His birth was announced to the shepherds (Luke 2.11), and for the same reason that His name was chosen (Matt. 1.21); and it was as a 'Ransom' that He regarded His forthcoming death (Mark 10.45): a sacrifice made in fulfilment of the Scriptural prophecies (Luke 24. 25–27) for the purpose of achieving for man the forgiveness of his sins (Matt. 26.28).

When we read the lives of most great people, their deaths are usually dismissed in the last few pages of the final chapter. But with Jesus it was different. As His last week approached, the narrative seems to slow up. The cameras which have roamed panoramically over His life home in upon the events, and focus on every little detail; so much so that we might almost call the gospel 'The death of Jesus, with prologue', rather than 'The life of Jesus, with epilogue'. Most people are remembered by their lives, but Jesus by His death; most men by what they achieved, but Jesus by what He suffered; most men by their action, but Jesus by His passion. And the supper which He instituted as a

memorial to Himself was not to recall some great and
miraculous triumph, but to commemorate His death and
passion.

And when we turn from the gospels to the epistles, we
find this same emphasis upon the cross. If you remove this
theme from the teaching of the apostles, you remove what
to them was the heart of the gospel, and indeed, you are left
with no gospel at all. Like the poet William Cowper, Paul
could say:

> E'er since by faith I saw the stream
>   Thy dying wounds supply,
> Redeeming love has been my theme
>   And shall be till I die.

There is a Nativity Play in which the child Jesus is made
to stand in the middle of the stage, and is approached from
either side by an angel. One angel offers Him a gorgeous
bouquet of roses, and the other a crown of thorns. The child
hesitates for a moment. He looks at the roses, fingers their
petals, enjoys their fragrance; and then with an almost im-
perceptible sigh, he takes the crown of thorns.

Just how soon Jesus began to realize what 'His Father's
business' involved, and where 'the will of God' would lead
Him, we cannot say. It is clear that at the time of His
temptation (Matt. 4) He set His face against other more
attractive options, and began to walk the *via dolorosa*
which, it must have become increasingly apparent to Him,
could have only one ending.

I have always thought that an interpretation of the
Temptation which sees it only as an attempt on Satan's part
to make Jesus gratify some physical desire or worldly ambition was too naïve and simplistic. If that had been the
case, Satan would surely have been wasting his time. It was
Jesus' methods rather than His motives which were Satan's
target – anything to make Jesus by-pass or avoid the cross.

'Why not become a great Economist?' suggested Satan.
'You could then use your miraculous powers to meet the
physical and social needs of suffering humanity. You know
you have power over nature. "Trees where you sit will crowd
into a shade." Command that these stones be turned into
bread.'

Again, 'Why not become a great Entertainer? Throw yourself down from the pinnacles of the temple, and walk away unharmed. Attract people to your teaching and to the love of God by some marvellous act of magic. The world loves to be diverted, and entertainers are ever among the most popular and best paid people in the world. Why not appeal to that side of human nature?

'Or if neither of these roles appeals to you, then what about becoming a great Emperor – another greater and better Alexander, Caesar, Napoleon, Stalin? At a nod from you all the kingdoms of the world will become yours, and you can lead the peoples where you will.'

We touch here upon one of the deep paradoxes of our religion. We know that it was Satan who caused the death of Jesus. It was he who 'entered into Judas Iscariot' (Luke 22.3). It was he who stirred up the people and inspired the high priests. And yet at the same time there was nothing he dreaded more or was more anxious to avoid than the cross. How can this be? Satan divided against himself? Precisely! He wanted to prevent the thing he most desired, and cause what he most feared. He wanted to destroy Jesus, but he knew that by doing so he would destroy himself.

We shall return to this theme of the crucifixion in a later chapter, and consider just how it was that upon the cross Jesus was able to achieve our forgiveness, but for the present we are concerned simply to note the centrality of the cross in the Christian Faith. It is a cross (not a cradle or even a crown) that has become the symbol of that faith, solely because of what Jesus did upon it nearly two thousand years ago. We see it in our churches, on our grave stones, round people's necks – decorated, bejewelled and beautified. But it was not always so. First invented by the Phoenicians, and lasting for a thousand years until it was finally abolished by the Emperor Constantine, it was probably the most brutal and inhumane form of execution ever invented by the ingenious cruelty of man; but because of what Jesus did there, it has been transformed into a thing of beauty.

Have you sometimes stood outside a very ordinary, perhaps even an ugly, building, and wondered why it is still allowed to stand in an area which is being developed and modernized? Then your eye has caught a plaque in one of the walls: 'So-and-so lived here', 'Such-and-such a book was written here', 'The King of Ruritania was born here'. Immediately that very common-or-garden house assumes a new significance and even a sanctity it never had before, and you understand why it has been preserved as a national monument. So it is with the cross. The most barbaric instrument of torture has become a thing of beauty, surpassingly precious to Christians who love to sing, not 'When I survey the *monstrous* cross', but 'When I survey the *wondrous* cross on which the Prince of Glory died'.

But we must turn to a third question, and ask *Where is He?* It is still possible in Moscow to pay a small fee, join a long queue, and file past a glass case containing the mummified remains of Lenin, the founder of Communism, one of the world's most popular religions. Other religions may be able to point to some shrine or tomb, but not so Christianity; for the most startling claim it makes for itself is that its Founder is alive. 'I am He that liveth and was dead; and behold I am alive for evermore' (Rev. 1.18); and those who came seeking His body on that first Easter morning received the breath-taking news, 'Why do you seek the living among the dead? He is not here, but He is risen' (Luke 24.5, 6).

We must be clear first of all what the Bible means by the resurrection. Jesus did not come back from death, like Jairus' daughter (Mark 5.33–35) or Lazarus (John 11.41–46), only to die again in a few years' time, sooner or later. Jesus passed through death and came out on the further side. He was not simply revived, that is, given the old life back again, but raised to a new kind of life altogether. The person who met the disciples during the next forty days was the same personality in a transformed body, so that while it was recognizably His, it was no longer subject to the same laws of nature.

But the proper habitat for this new resurrection body was not, and could never be, this earth, and that is why after those forty days He returned to heaven. But first it was necessary to demonstrate the fact that He was unmistakably alive, and by coming and going among His disciples in unexpected ways to train them to enjoy His presence with them by faith rather than by sight.

But can we genuinely believe in a resurrection of this sort today? Are there not simpler and more credible explanations of what took place?

To begin with we have got to explain the appearances of Jesus to His disciples. They were not credulous or gullible men. In fact, they were the very reverse. They did not expect to see Him. For them Good Friday had spelt the end of all their hopes. Moreover, while we can imagine that one or two of them might have suffered some sort of hallucination, the remarkable thing is how often He appeared to a whole group of His followers at once – on one occasion to as many as five hundred (1 Cor. 15.6) – and it is unthinkable that they could all have been mistaken.

We might be forced into an explanation of this sort if the authorities had been able to produce the body of Jesus, which had been carefully guarded over the weekend. But not only were they unable to do so, they actually had to invent a very limp story by saying that while the soldiers slept, the disciples came and stole the body, and then launched the myth of a resurrection.

But not only is there nothing in the narrative to suggest this possibility, but it is totally out of character with what we know of the disciples. Did they really possess the courage and initiative for such a daring action? Did no one see them do it and try to prevent them? Did no one leak the story? And where did they dispose of the body? Moreover, if we accept this theory (which even the authorities themselves did not believe but only invented) are we really to suppose that a cowardly little group of peasants were so transformed by the deceit which they had perpetrated that within a few weeks they were being accused of turning the world upside down with their teaching (Acts 17.6) and gladly accepting imprisonment and even martyrdom, all for the sake of a lie? People will maintain a hoax for a little while, but they won't go to those lengths.

With what then are we left? We need not take seriously the suggestion that the women who were first on the scene mistook the tomb in the early morning light (someone would have quickly corrected their mistake), or that Jesus was not really dead, and revived sufficiently in the tomb to make His escape, presumably to die at a later date. Nor need we allow the apparent discrepancies in the narrative to disturb us. In fact the reverse is true, for a complete harmonization of the four accounts would have suggested a degree of connivance which would have been highly suspicious.

No! It is a matter of plain logic that when you have found every possible natural explanation for an event unacceptable, then you are obliged to turn to the supernatural, and all that remains for us to do is to believe the unvarnished incredible truth that 'on the third day Jesus rose again from the dead'.

I have always been interested in the different approach to the subject of the resurrection that we find between the early disciples and ourselves. We are always at great pains to do what I have just been trying to do, to prove that the resurrection was an historical fact. But the disciples were more interested in showing what the resurrection itself proved. In other words, we tend to say, 'If Jesus rose from the dead, then He must be the Son of God', but in their early preaching in the Acts they argued the other way round: 'Because He was the Son of God He must have risen from the dead, for "it was not possible that death should keep Him in its grip".' (Acts 2.24). To the disciples the resurrection of Jesus was such a proven, impregnable fact, that they did not need to argue about it. They assumed it was true, and went on from there.

But as I have said, the natural environment for the risen Christ was not earth, but heaven, and it could only be a matter of time before He returned there. The forty days served to teach His disciples that He was not only alive, but always present and available. This was of great importance, because before long they would be proclaiming the message to thousands who had never seen Him in the flesh, and for whom faith was therefore the only possible way of experiencing His presence. As Peter himself was to write to such people, 'Whom having not seen, ye love: in whom, though now ye see Him not, yet believing, ye rejoice with joy unspeakable' (1 Pet. 1.8).

Forty days were considered long enough for this exercise, and then Jesus took His departure, and in the simple words of the narrative, 'while they watched, He was taken up; and a cloud received Him out of their sight' (Acts 1.9). I remember how this experience was brought home to me when once I stood in a circle while some royal personage was taken from our midst in a helicopter. We were left gazing heavenwards until he disappeared from sight, and then looking at each other across the yawning gap he had left.

Critics have made great play with the fact that the ascension of Jesus seems to assume an outmoded view of the universe, with its idea of heaven being 'up there' and hell 'down there'; but it always seems to me that this sort of objection to the vertical take-off which Jesus made is rather juvenile. To the simple people He was concerned with, 'up' was always symbolic, as indeed it is to us, of promotion and glory; while had He departed in some horizontal fashion, over a distant horizon, they might have thought He was merely visiting another continent. How, I would like to ask these modern sceptics, would they have arranged His departure?

And it is in heaven, seated at the right hand of God, that we must think of the bodily presence of Jesus today (Col. 3.1). We are told that 'He must be received into heaven until the time of universal restoration comes' (Acts 3.21). But why the 'must'? First of all for the very simple reason that if He were still on earth He could only be in one place at a time. Let us suppose that He chose to reside in Jerusalem or Nazareth. Then very quickly an impossible situation would arise as millions of pilgrims tried to force their way into His presence. Jesus Himself foresaw this. 'It is for your good that I am leaving you,' He said (John 16.7), 'but though I am leaving you, I am not deserting you, for I will send the Holy Spirit to take my place and make me universally available to my followers.'

An illustration may help. Suppose someone in your town or village, your office or your school, were to become world-famous overnight. How he does it must be left to your imagination, but through some invention, discovery of achievement this person's name becomes a household word, on everyone's lips, and adorning with banner headlines every newspaper.

Very quickly an impossible situation arises, and things get completely out of hand, as people from all over the world begin to pour into the neighbourhood by road, rail and air. Life comes to a complete standstill, as millions try to get a glimpse of this great celebrity.

It is then, we will suppose, that the BBC steps in. A helicopter lands conveniently near, the person is bundled

into it, and whisked off to the television studios. You and
I who have struggled into the area hoping for a photograph
and even an autograph, feel cheated and disappointed. Just
when we hoped to enjoy him, he was snatched from our
presence.

But I think we would see the sense of what had taken
place if that night, on a programme like Nationwide, this
famous person were to speak to the whole country. We
would realize that he had been taken away from the few
that he might be given back to the many: absent from some
in the body, he became available for all in the spirit. Of
course there would be those who through prejudice, pre-
occupation or just lack of interest would want nothing to do
with him; but others, many others, would switch on to him,
and feel that they were enjoying his presence almost as really
as if he were physically in their midst.

We shall return to this subject in the next chapter, but
it is important at this stage to understand the relationship
between Jesus and the Holy Spirit. Jesus as a physical
person was local; the Holy Spirit made Him available. Jesus was
like the light of the sun; the Holy Spirit was its warmth,
permeating the hearts of believers everywhere and for all
time (Rom. 5.5). Or, to change the metaphor, Jesus was the
form of the flowers, which we admire as we see them on the
table; the Holy Spirit was their fragrance which filled the
whole room. The two are distinct and yet inseparable.

But there was a second reason why Jesus 'must' return to
heaven, and that was that He might represent us in the
presence of God. He is our advocate, pleading our cause on
account of His death upon the cross. It is interesting to note
that John uses the same word (Greek – *paracleetos*, 1 John
2.1) about Jesus as Jesus Himself uses of the Holy Spirit
(John 16.7). For just as the Holy Spirit represents the
Father to us, pleading His cause, and drawing men to
Himself, so Jesus represents us to the Father.

In this way, therefore, we must think of Jesus – seated,
because His work is done; and seated in the place of honour,
at the right hand of the Father, 'until the time of universal
restoration comes'. When will that time be? And what will
happen?

When will He return? Few facts receive greater prominence or emphasis in the New Testament than the return of

Christ to this earth; and it is one which has therefore quite properly found its way into all the Christian Creeds. Along with all the other facts that we have been considering, we are invited to state our belief that 'He shall come again with glory to judge both the quick and the dead: whose kingdom shall have no end.'

And it is these two things that Christ will come to do: to judge and to reign. It seems that there will be two kinds of judgement. The first will distinguish believers from unbelievers, and people will be judged according to their attitude to Christ, and their response to His claims (John 3.18, 5.24; 2 Thess. 1.7–10): whether they have believed in Him and obéyed His gospel, or whether they have rejected Him.

The exact position of the heathen and of those who have had no chance to hear or understand the gospel is unclear, and we are left, perhaps deliberately, with no definite indication as to their destiny. It seems that there is no excuse on the part of many for failing to make some response to what God has revealed of Himself through nature and in their own conscience (Rom. 1.19, 20); but at the same time, the responsibility of those who have had the full light of the gospel must be far greater than of those who have lived in semi-darkness, who have never heard of Christ, or who through some mental deficiency or handicap have never had the chance to reach an understanding of the truth. But we shall consider this subject more fully in a later chapter.

The second kind of judgement concerns Christians, and the question this time is not whether we believe, but how we behave. The famous parable of the talents (Matt. 25.15–30) seems to be intended to teach this lesson; and Paul takes up the same theme in his letter to the Corinthians (1 Cor. 3.11–15). In other words, there are 'Christians and Christians', 'O' Level and 'A' Level Christians; and while a place in heaven will be assured to all, there will be special rewards and responsibilities for those whose lives have been truly Christlike, and who will not be ashamed at the coming of Christ, because they have been wholly dedicated to His service (1 John 2.28; 2 Tim. 2.15).

And Jesus will return to reign. The Old Testament picture of a kingdom of everlasting righteousness (Isa. 35), which some had mistakenly expected Him to establish at His first

coming will finally become a reality, 'and He shall reign for
ever and ever' (Rev. 11.15); and it seems likely that the
prelude, the overture to this eternal reign will begin here
on earth and be continued in heaven.

The precise programme or time-table of the events concerning the return of Christ is not for us to know. We are
deliberately kept in ignorance (Matt. 24.36). Indeed, it is
not always easy to decipher our Lord's own teaching on the
subject, and to know whether He is speaking of His own
return or of the fall of Jerusalem which took place within
the life-time of many who knew Him here on earth. The two
events, like mountains seen from a distance, often appear to
be much closer together than they really are, and almost
merge into each other.

What we may confidently assert is that the coming of the
Lord will be unexpected (Matt. 24.43; Rev. 16.15), and at
the same time unmistakable (1 Thes. 4.16). In these
respects it will differ from His first coming. On Christmas
Day the King landed, so to speak, in disguise on enemy-
occupied territory. Few knew He had come or recognized
Him. Next time His coming will be a triumphant invasion.
We do not know when it will happen, but just as there were
astute and observant members of the French Resistance
Movement who knew in 1944 that the liberation of their
country could not be very long delayed, so to the spiritually
discerning Christian there will be, and perhaps already are,
signs which will tell him that the coming of the Lord draws
near (2 Tim. 3.1–4; 2 Pet. 3.3, 4).

3 The Holy Spirit

It is clear from many parts of the Bible that the Holy Spirit is to be thought of as a Person. To suggest that He is an influence or an atmosphere, rather in the same way that we talk about 'the spirit of Christmas' or 'the team spirit' is to fail completely to do justice to the language of the Old and New Testaments alike. He is frequently spoken of as Counsellor, Strengthener or Advocate, and it is impossible to think of such words except as they relate to a definite person.

It was not for many years after the ascension of Christ that what is called the doctrine of the Trinity, the belief that there are three distinct persons in one God, was explicitly defined; but the implication of that doctrine is very clear from many parts of the Bible (Matt. 28.19). To begin with there are three distinct Persons to whom at different times are attributed divine powers, and yet who are related in such a way that they can only be described as a unity; and again there are three ways in which men and women seem to enjoy an encounter with God – through creation (the Father), redemption (the Son) and experience (the Holy Spirit).

It is here perhaps that an analogy will help us. Think for a moment of any book with which you are familiar – *War and Peace*, perhaps, or *Treasure Island*. That book can exist in three quite separate and distinct ways, and yet ways which are intimately related and concurrent.

First, it exists in the mind of the author. Long before it takes physical shape and form, and becomes, so to speak, 'flesh', it is there in its entirety, and if asked to do so, the author could produce the whole story from his head.

Then, secondly, there comes the 'incarnation', when the idea is embodied in written form, and the book takes actual shape as a volume. It becomes something that 'we can see with our eyes, which we can look upon, and our hands handle' (1 John 1.1). *Treasure Island*, for instance, is not just a disembodied story. It is something I can point to in a particular room, on a particular shelf in a book case.

In the third place the book exists in the imagination of the reader. The title 'Treasure Island' will conjure up a whole range of mental images and pictures. I may possess it in my mind and feed upon it in my imagination. Indeed, even if I do not possess the book in material form at all, I may carry it about with me wherever I go, because I have made what was an historical event a personal experience.

The application of this analogy is obvious, and needs no development, but there is one important caveat which must be entered. In the case of the book, there is a sort of sequence: the idea, then the incarnation, then the imagination; but in the case of the Trinity it is important to remember that all three Persons existed from the beginning. That is to say, there never was a time when there was just God alone.

What happened on Christmas Day, and then again on the Day of Pentecost, was not that Jesus, the Son, and then the Holy Spirit came into existence. These were the occasions on which these two Persons of the Trinity made their formal entry into the world and into the affairs of men. They had been there, to use John's phrase, 'in the bosom of the Father' (John 1.18) from all eternity. Historically they 'proceeded from the Father' (and the Son), rather as a telescope is extended, first by one concealed section and then another.

The work of the Holy Spirit in the Old Testament seems to have been spasmodic and intermittent rather than continuous. We find Him associated with God in the creation of man (Gen. 2.7) and indeed of the whole world (Gen. 1.2); while it is He who sustains and refreshes life upon earth (Psa. 104.30).

There are times too when for some special purpose He came upon men and women, endowing them with supernatural strength for some special task, giving them power (Judg. 14.6), courage (Judg. 3.10) or wisdom (Ex. 31.3); while it is He who provides the motive and the strength for people to live according to the will of God (Psa. 51 and 139).

Finally, we are told that it was the Holy Spirit who inspired the prophets (2 Pet. 1.21), often leading them to speak of mysteries, such as the future coming of the Messiah, of which they only had the faintest understanding, and were ministering not to the spiritual advantage of their own generation, but ours (1 Pet. 1.10–12).

It is important to remember that these three functions of the Holy Spirit were not discontinued with the coming of Christ, but were simply translated into New Testament terms. Thus it is the Holy Spirit who brings about the new creation (2 Cor. 5.17), the re-birth of man (John 3.5); it is His power which produces moral and spiritual maturity in the life of the Christian believer (Ga. 5.22, 23); and it is He again who reveals to us and interprets the deep things of God (1 Cor. 2.9, 10) and the teaching of the Bible. He continues to be Creator, Strengthener and Interpreter.

When we come to the New Testament, we find that the Holy Spirit is closely associated with many of the important events in the early part of Jesus' life, before He was fully launched upon His ministry. He is the agent at His birth (Luke 1.35), present at His baptism (Matt. 3.13–17) and temptation (Matt. 4.1–11) and equips and prepares Him for His work (Luke 4.14–18). But though Jesus often spoke of Him, and looked forward to the time when He would be fully outpoured upon His church (John 16.5–14), His activity in the gospels was obviously limited by the fact that at that time Jesus was living and working amongst His disciples (John 7.39).

It was on the Day of Pentecost that what has been called 'the age of the Spirit' really began. On that day 'the promise of the Father' (Acts 1.4) was fulfilled, and the Holy Spirit was poured out upon the believers as they were gathered together in Jerusalem (Acts 2.1–4). What precisely had He come to do? There are many metaphors in the New Testament which are used to describe the work of the Holy Spirit, but perhaps three are of particular importance and deserve special attention.

First of all, He is an *Ambassador*. We saw this in the last chapter. Just as Jesus is an ambassador for us in the court of heaven, so the Holy Spirit represents Him in the heart of the believer; and just as it is impossible for the Queen to be personally present in all the capitals of the world, so Jesus, now seated at the right hand of God, is represented on earth by the Holy Spirit.

It is the ambassador's task to make known the mind, the

will and the purpose of the government he represents: to
rebuke, encourage, warn or advise as the case may be. And
this is what the Holy Spirit does for the Christian.

> And His that gentle voice we hear
>   Soft as the breath of even,
> That checks each fault and calms each fear,
>   And speaks of heaven.

But how do we recognize His voice amidst the noisy
clamour of so many others that demand our attention? The
answer is that what He says will always be consistent with
the teaching we have received from Jesus Himself. It is not
the task of the Holy Spirit to initiate new truth, but rather
to underline and interpret existing truth.

The relationship which exists between the Holy Spirit
and the Word of God might be compared with that which
exists between the light which illumines Big Ben and the
clock itself. Big Ben tells us the time. It gives us the truth;
but during the night that truth is revealed and brought home
to us by the light inside. 'Truth' and 'Spirit' go together.
Truth without Spirit produces knowledge but no life (2 Cor.
3.6), and the Spirit without the Truth will produce life
without knowledge. It is the task of the Holy Spirit 'not to
speak of Himself' (that is, on His own authority), but to
bring to the heart and mind and conscience of the Christian
believer the things that Jesus has taught and said (John
14–16).

In the second place we must think of the Holy Spirit as
a *Benefactor*. He bestows gifts upon Christians, the gifts they
need for serving Christ, and He equips them with the power
they need to witness for Him. What these gifts are may be
discovered from a study of 1 Corinthians 12 and 14. It must
be said at once that Christians differ in their interpretation
of these passages and in their understanding of the nature
of some of these gifts. Is the gift of 'tongues' some form of
ecstatic utterance or the ability to speak in languages that
have never been learned? Is 'prophecy' a message directly
and immediately imparted by God, or the exposition of
truth otherwise revealed? Again, are all the gifts to be
understood in exactly the same terms as in the first century
AD? Were some bestowed for a special, local and perhaps

even temporary purpose and have since become obsolete? Or
are they all of universal and eternal application?

It must in fairness be admitted that the controversy this
matter has engendered has been keen and even at times
acrimonious, though it now appears to be subsiding, as a
much more tolerant attitude begins to prevail amongst the
vast majority of fair-minded Christians. We shall return to
this subject at the end of the chapter, but what may now be
said without contradiction is that the Holy Spirit is continuing to endow some Christians with special gifts. What
else can account for the remarkable power of some preachers,
for the wisdom of others as counsellors, for the faith of
others in prayer, and for the clear-headed administrative
ability of those who create the framework for so much
spiritual advance?

But while Paul acknowledged the existence and use of
spiritual gifts, and indeed exercised them himself, he was
always at pains to point out the far greater value in God's
eyes of virtues; and it is significant that, sandwiched between
1 Corinthians 12 and 14 we have the famous 'Poem of Love'
in Chapter 13, which he describes in another place as the
primary 'fruit of the Spirit' (Gal. 5.22, 23). In his eyes the
Christian is not only a 'Christmas tree', laden with gifts,
but also a 'fruit tree', producing the luscious and desirable
virtues of love, joy, peace, long-suffering and so on. If we
lack these things, then the value of eloquence, prophecy and
all the other gifts are rendered hollow and invalid.

Thirdly we are taught that the Holy Spirit is a *Comforter*.
In our ears this word conveys the idea of luxury and ease.
We have further debased its value by contracting it to its
diminutive 'comfy'. 'Do have a comfy chair,' we say to a
visitor. But this is not its real meaning. It is related to such
words as 'fortify' and 'fortress', and has a much stronger
and more virile origin. In the Bayeux Tapestry there is a
scene depicted in which William of Normandy is seen
prodding one of his soldiers in the backside with a sword,
and underneath are the words, 'William comforteth one of
his soldiers' – the kind of comfort most of us would think
twice about receiving. Lord Coggan in an article suggested
that a better word would be 'Stimulator'.

Literally, of course, the Greek word *paracleetos* means
one who is 'called alongside'; and the Latin equivalent

advocatus gives us our English word 'advocate', or 'counsel for the defence'. It is important to note that so far as the world is concerned, the Holy Spirit is 'Counsel for the prosecution', for it is His task to secure conviction of sin in the heart of the unbeliever (John 16.8, 9); but for the Christian He plays the part of the 'prisoner's friend', coming to our aid as a barrister does to a defendant, or a tug to a ship in difficulty or distress.

More particularly, He assists us when we are assailed by doubts (Rom. 8.16), for it is He who re-assures us deep down in our hearts that we belong to Christ. It is He who strengthens us against temptation of every kind (Eph. 3.16). And it is He too who helps us in our prayers (Rom. 8.26), bringing to our minds the things for which we ought to pray, inspiring us to pray when perhaps we least feel like doing so, and indeed 'editing' our prayers, and presenting them to the Father on our behalf.

When you think about it, it is clear that the Holy Spirit performs all the operations which Jesus performed while He was on earth. The work of Jesus is carried on by the Holy Spirit, and perhaps the most helpful way of thinking of Him is to think of the life and work of Jesus extended, so to speak, into a spiritual dimension.

When, for instance, someone speaks of 'receiving Christ' (Rev. 3.20) or 'coming to Him' (Matt. 11.28) what in effect happens is that the Holy Spirit quite literally begins to 'dwell in our hearts by faith' (Eph. 3.17). This theme of 'the indwelling Spirit' is one to which Paul and the other writers of the New Testament refer frequently. They also speak on a number of occasions of being 'filled with the Spirit' (Acts 13.9), meaning that He is allowed access into every room in the heart of the believer, an experience which of course depends directly upon the degree of our own personal surrender.

A friend comes to stay, we will imagine, and as time goes on he so captivates and charms us, that we regard him as 'one of the family'. We beg him to 'make himself at home', to 'come and go as he likes'. He began by dwelling, but he ends by filling the house with the beauty and radiance of his presence. That is how it should be with the Holy Spirit.

The coming of the Holy Spirit on the Day of Pentecost was accompanied by two very suggestive symbols – wind and

fire (Acts 2.1–4), two of the great elemental forces of nature.
They have three things in common: their sovereignty, their
mystery and their energy. So it is with the Holy Spirit. We
cannot dictate to Him or control Him. We can never fully
understand how He works in the world. We can set no limit
to what He can do in the hearts and lives of men and women,
or suppose that anyone is beyond His reach or outside the
sphere of His influence.

But just as people opposed Jesus while He was on earth,
so it is possible for us to hinder and frustrate the work of
the Holy Spirit, both in our own hearts and in the world at
large.

It is possible, for example, to '*resist* the Holy Spirit'. This
is what Stephen charged his accusers of doing (Acts 7.51),
and it is what Saul of Tarsus was doing when we read that
he was 'kicking against the pricks' (Acts 9.5). It means that
we refuse to accept the instruction and guidance of the
Holy Spirit, and insist upon going our own way, and so to
speak, 'walking against the wind'. The Holy Spirit will
frequently try to guide us, using the Bible, our own conscience and perhaps the advice of Christian friends to indicate the way He would like us to go. The secret of
happiness in the Christian life is to learn the art of instant
obedience. If on the other hand, we adopt the opposite
attitude, resisting the persuasion of His 'still small voice',
then we must not be surprised if in time we cease to hear it
altogether; for even the Holy Spirit cannot teach the un-
teachable, or guide those who are not willing to be led.

Then it is possible to '*quench* the Holy Spirit' (1 Thess.
5.19). The quickest way to put out a fire is to deprive it of
oxygen, and it is possible so to fill our lives with other things,
often quite right and proper in their place, that the Holy
Spirit has no room to breathe, His influence is stifled, and
the fire which He lit in our hearts, and which once burned
so brightly, is almost extinguished. Far from allowing it to
be quenched in this way, we must do all in our power to
feed and nourish the flames, welcoming all the fuel we can
receive from the Bible, from Christian literature and the
help of Christian friends.

It has been said that the Holy Spirit is very sensitive,
because by resisting the wind and quenching the fire what
we are doing in effect is to 'grieve' a friend (Eph. 4.30); for

by entertaining in our lives things which we know He dislikes, we hurt and displease Him. The good host would never allow himself to behave in this way to an honoured guest. The menu, the programme, the other guests would all be chosen with a view to making him feel perfectly at home. To behave otherwise towards Christ will not, it is true, drive Him from our lives, but it will make Him ill at ease, and have the effect, so to speak, of 'confining Him to His room', so that His influence, which could make such a difference for good, is restricted and diluted.

*   *   *

Before leaving this chapter on the Holy Spirit, it is necessary to discuss in some detail what is referred to as 'the baptism of the Holy Spirit'. There are several references to it in the New Testament (Acts 1.5; 11.16, etc), and it is thought by many Christians to refer to an experience which takes place after conversion, which depends upon a complete surrender of the Christian to God, and which is followed (some would say invariably) by an endowment with certain gifts of the Holy Spirit which, as we have already seen, are listed for us in 1 Corinthians 12 and 14.

For many years before this more recent and post-war emphasis upon spiritual renewal, there have been Christians who have taught the necessity of what used to be called 'the second blessing'. It formed part of Dr Torrey's teaching, and was closely associated with the Keswick Convention in its earlier days. You needed what one speaker used to call 'the second sixpence', a reference perhaps to the 'King's Shilling' which used to be given to those who enlisted in the armed services. This 'second blessing' was again dependent upon full surrender to God, and followed by a fresh release of power, though in those days very little was heard of the gifts of the Spirit.

Now there can be no doubt that this teaching corresponded to the experience of a great many Christians. It was only after conversion, perhaps months or even years later, that they saw the full implications of following Christ. Like the Children of Israel, they had been delivered from Egypt, but they were not yet in the Promised Land. Their unsatisfactory and fruitless 'wilderness experience' could only be ended by a full and glad surrender of themselves to God.

But how far Christian leaders were right in insisting upon the automatic necessity of this step as a normal experience, is more doubtful, for it threw some into confusion, because they did not know where they stood, and I can remember a certain agitation on this subject in the Cambridge Camp at Keswick in 1937.

It was not one of the well-known platform speakers who cleared my own thinking on this subject, but the ex-army cook who was providing for our needs in the camp. 'What the blood has cleansed', he said to me in the course of a conversation, 'the Spirit fills.' The Holy Spirit, if we may say so, abhors a vacuum, and will therefore always fill us to the level of our repentance and cleansing. But of course there is no guarantee that if I am completely filled today, I shall be completely filled tomorrow.

My own thinking and study in this subject has therefore led me to the conclusion that the 'baptism of the Holy Spirit' is something which takes place at conversion, when we receive Him into our hearts by faith; but the fullness of the Holy Spirit is a day-to-day experience, and depends upon just how much of my heart and life I make available for Him to fill.

Turning to this more recent phenomenon, to what is sometimes loosely called 'the charismatic movement', I find that this same sort of confusion exists. I believe it is due to a minority of Christian teachers who insist upon what they feel is the Scriptural necessity of an experience which has obviously meant much to them, but who regard all those who have not enjoyed it as in some sense deficient and even 'second-class Christians'. It is only right to add that there are a great many who have had this experience, and who do not take this 'hard line'. They realize that God does not deal with all His children in the same way, nor distribute His gifts evenly throughout the whole church; and while the experience may mean a great deal to them personally, it does not form an integral part of their teaching, and in all humility they are able to look up to those with whom God has dealt differently. They follow the Scriptural instruction laid down by Paul in another context, 'Keep what you believe about this matter, then, between yourself and God' (Rom. 14.22).

On the other hand the problem has been to some extent aggravated by the fact that some Christians have seemingly elevated the gift of tongues on to a plane by itself, as the most important of all. This is curious when we remember how Paul himself tried to minimise its importance when describing the gifts at the disposal of the Holy Spirit, and stressed the fact that they were distributed in such a way that no Christian should feel deprived if his particular gift was not the same as the man's next door; for the whole point and purpose of the gifts of the Spirit and their distribution was to provide variety of activity and function within the unity of the body of the Church (1 Cor. 12).

On a more general level there are I think several things which can usefully be said. First, we must not assume that the circumstances of every New Testament event can be translated into personal experiences today. Many of these were 'one off' events and quite unique.

For example, the coming of the Holy Spirit on the Day of Pentecost was a unique, never-to-be-repeated historical occurrence. The 'rushing mighty wind' and 'the tongues of fire' were phenomena it would be quite unreasonable to expect again; and the gift of languages which immediately followed, which showed that the curse of Babel had been reversed (Gen. 11) and the original 'unity of the Spirit' restored, has, so far as we know, never happened in that form or on that scale again.

Nor may we regard as typical the events at Samaria (Acts 8.14–17) and Ephesus (Acts 19.1–7). These people lived in that curious twilight between the Old and New Testaments in which Simeon (Luke 2.25), Cornelius (Acts 10.1, 2) and others 'waited for the kingdom of God'. Their very special condition called for unusual treatment, and what was done to meet particular historical circumstances which were never repeated cannot be accepted as normal practice or experience today.

In the second place we must be careful not to make a doctrine out of an experience. This, I believe, has been the mistake of some of the Christian teachers to whom I have referred. There is a temptation to suppose that if an experience is vivid enough, and if it is shared by a sufficiently large number if Christians, then it will automatically qualify as a dogma. In her fascinating book *I dared to call Him*

Father, Bilquis Sheikh tells us of some remarkable dreams which she had and by which she was convinced that God was speaking to her. We need not for a moment doubt this. But it would be a dangerous mistake to suppose that God must necessarily use this method, or that we can trace His voice in every dream. This way heresy lies. Scripture always works in the opposite direction. Experience is distilled from dogma, and not vice versa.

Thirdly we need to remember that there are many parts of Scripture about which even the most sincere Christians will differ as to their interpretation, and on which it is presumptuous to suppose that anyone this side of heaven will have the last word. Most readers will be familiar with the controversy which has raged over such matters as the precise nature of church government, the Second Coming, the role of women in the Church and so on. There are many issues on which the Christian must maintain an attitude of reverent agnosticism. We simply do not know the final answer. Perhaps it is God's way of keeping us humble. He obliges us to say, 'This is how I understand it', rather than 'I know I am right'. This is very much to the point so far as the gifts of the Holy Spirit are concerned. There is so much that we do not, and probably never will know, that one man's experience must not necessarily be used to condemn another man's lack of it, nor vice versa.

Finally, it is a mistake to suppose that there is more than one experience in the Christian life which is irreversible. There is not. The only irreversible experience is by definition the New Birth; for you cannot be 'unborn'. But so far as the rest is concerned, the teaching of the Bible seems to suggest that we never reach a point from which it is not possible to slip back: a fact which is often overlooked by those who place too much emphasis upon a 'second blessing'.

As we have already seen, we are taught in the New Testament that the Holy Spirit dwells in the heart of every Christian believer, but His sovereignty and sway depend upon a daily yielding of ourselves to His influence, and it is therefore an experience which cannot be guaranteed in perpetuity, but only moment by moment. In other words, what some call 'the fullness of the Spirit' and others 'the baptism of the Spirit' is not a once-for-all experience, but rather the result of a perpetually maintained attitude of trust and obedience towards God: a renewal which I need afresh every day of my life.

4 Man

It was Blaise Pascal (1623–1662) who described man as 'the glory and the scandal of the universe'; and it would hardly have been possible to have summed up the character of human nature more aptly or completely than that.

Looked at in one way we are what has been called 'nature's masterpiece', clearly the most remarkable thing in existence, capable of quite astonishing technological inventions and discoveries, and of producing the most sublime poetry, music and art. 'What a piece of work is man! how noble in reason! how infinite in faculty; in form, in moving, how express and admirable! in action how like an angel! in apprehension how like a god! The beauty of the world! the paragon of animals!'

All that is true, and represents one view of ourselves, but there is another, darker side to this picture; for man is capable of the most bestial behaviour, and has left behind him down the centuries a trail of misery and desolation. It is doubtful whether even Shakespeare, if he had lived in different circumstances, or perhaps in this century rather than in the sixteenth century, and had known more of 'man's inhumanity to man', would have been able to write in such glowing terms. We cannot escape the melancholy reflection that the world might be a much better place without the human race, 'for every prospect pleases, and only man is vile'.

But we will begin by thinking of what might be called the *dignity of man* – man, that is to say, as God intended him to be; and in this regard the Bible has three important things to say. First, it tells us that we are *made by God*. Whatever poetical gloss some modern scholars may like to put upon the opening chapters of Genesis, the underlying truth remains that man is seen there to be the result of God's direct intervention, and the climax of His creative process. It was only after man had appeared on the scene, that 'everything that God had made' was declared to be '*very* good', and only then that He felt able to desist from His work and rest (Gen. 1.26–31).

And this fact, that man is created by God, is taken up throughout Scripture. In Psalm 139, for example, the writer says, 'I am fearfully and wonderfully made', and he goes on to speak of his Maker as one who understands him completely, and who knows just how his mind and his body work and indeed one of the most interesting things about the Bible is its astonishingly accurate diagnosis of human nature, and the way in which it can be used as a kind of 'Maker's Handbook'.

And the fact that God made us, and 'made us', as the psalmist says, 'a little lower than the angels and has crowned us with glory and honour' (Psa. 8.5), means that we should look upon our fellow men and women with reverence and respect. The divine hall-mark is upon us all, giving us a dignity and a value which we would not otherwise possess.

But the Bible also insists that we are *made like God*, 'in His own image' (Gen. 1.26) and 'after His similitude' (Jas. 3.9). We are not therefore to suppose that we bear any physical resemblance to our Maker, and the Bible nowhere commits us to such a view. In fact, physically we are more 'like the beasts that perish' (Psa. 49.12). The likeness of which the Bible speaks is a moral and a spiritual one.

But what precisely does this mean? We thought just now of certain 'hall-marks', and it might be worth noting those things which make man in some sense a 'partaker of the divine nature', and which distinguish him from even the highest and most advanced animals.

First, there is what is sometimes called man's soul or his spirit. These words are not used in the Bible in a precise or technical sense, and their meaning varies from place to place. But we are referring here to that part of man's nature which is capable of apprehending God and communicating with Him: that part of our nature, if you like, which overlaps with His, and which therefore allows us to think of Him and to address Him in personal terms.

Secondly, man has a conscience. There is within all of us an innate sense of right and wrong, a sort of moral barometer which, though often misused and maladjusted, distinguishes however faintly and in even the most depraved, between good and evil. Conscience has been called 'the echo of God's voice', and it is doubtful whether there is anyone in whom it is completely absent. It is man's capacity to say 'I ought' and not just 'I want' that identifies him with God and distinguishes him from the rest of the animal creation.

Thirdly, man has freewill. He is a responsible being. Animals are controlled and governed largely, if not entirely, by instinct, but man has the power to rise above the obvious and instinctive course of action, and follow a line which is dictated by conscience or reason. Not only therefore is he made in such a way that he can distinguish between right and wrong, but he is endowed with the faculty for choosing the one and refusing the other.

The third and crowning aspect of man's dignity is that he is *made for God* (Isa. 43.21). 'O God,' cried St Augustine, 'Thou hast made us for Thyself, and our hearts are restless until they find repose in Thee.' But why did God make us?

In the first place He made us so that we might act as His 'Viceroy' on this planet, subduing and cultivating the earth (Gen. 1.28); and this seems to suggest that all proper research and exploration, conducted to His glory, are in line with His original intention and purpose for mankind.

But in the second place, and more importantly, He made us that He might enjoy our company and fellowship. God, in other words, did not make us for our own sake, but for His. As the writer of the Book of Revelation puts it, 'Thou hast created all things, and for Thy pleasure they are and were created' (Rev. 4.11). The crowning glory of man is just that: we exist to give pleasure to God, for there is a sense in which even He is incomplete without creatures on whom He may bestow His love and care and who are capable of responding to Him.

It follows as a matter of course that we can only find true happiness and meaning in life if we respond to God, and if we allow the relationship between us to exist. For man belongs to that class of objects whose existence only makes sense when it is related to something else. The electric light bulb, for example, or the LP disc have no meaning or purpose unless they are connected with the source of power which will produce light and sound; and for man too, apart from his relationship with God, there is no real purpose in existence. It is like the master and the dog we thought of in an earlier chapter. The master buys the dog because he wants the pleasure of a companion; and the dog responds to the master because this is the only way in which he will find true satisfaction in life.

Chapter two in the history of mankind must be entitled the *decline of man*. It tells the sad, familiar story of our disobedience, our 'unilateral declaration of independence' which, even if it had been successful, would have still constituted rebellion against God and against His laws.

The Bible has very little to say about the origin of evil. It starts by assuming its existence, but at the same time its absence from the world God had made and from the life of man. In other words, it was not endemic in God's creation, but an intrusion from without. It seems, from hints in certain parts of the Bible, that we are safe in assuming some sort of pre-cosmic fall involving the angels, when there was a rebellion among the heavenly beings attending God, to the chief amongst whom was given the name of Satan, meaning 'the adversary'.

He is introduced to us in the earliest chapters of Genesis in the form of a serpent, though it is obvious that this is only one of his many disguises. His malign influence is evident throughout Scripture, for it is his purpose to lead man into disobedience and sin, and thereby drive a wedge between him and his Maker.

Of course it would have been possible for God to have made man in such a way that he was incapable of sin. He could have created us as puppets or automata, able only to respond to the divine impulses exerted by God Himself. But we cannot believe for a moment that such creatures would have brought any pleasure to a God of love. The attribute of freewill, even though it carried with it the risk that it would be misused, was the only way in which there could be the sort of loving response that a father looks for in his children.

We are bound to believe too that in some way which we cannot at present perceive, and in the final analysis, even human sin and disobedience will contribute to the glory of God. An ancient Missal, in its *Exsultet* contains the startling sentence, *'O felix culpa, quae talem ac tantum meruit habere Redemptorem'* ('O happy sin, which has deserved to have such and so mighty a Redeemer'). But if it can be argued, as we shall try to do later, that a world without suffering and pain might not allow the existence of such noble virtues as courage and compassion, may we not extend that argument to include even sin; for 'where sin abounded, grace did much more abound' (Rom. 5.20)?

But we are moving into speculative regions, and must return to consider the immediate and melancholy consequences of sin. Quite apart from its effect upon man, it seems clear from Scripture that the whole of creation was dislocated and in some way involved in our Fall, and is even now 'groaning' for its final release from bondage (Rom. 8.19–22).

So far as man himself is concerned, the effect of sin has been to tarnish, blur and disfigure the image in which he was originally created. Like a Victorian penny, the features are just discernible, but often only dimly and faintly so. Sin has distorted man's *conscience*. It is like a clock which is so unreliable that it gives only a very rough indication of the time, and no longer with the precision which is required for satisfactory living.

And then again, it has enslaved man's *freewill*. Jesus said that he who commits sin becomes the servant or the slave of sin (John 8.34); and all too often even when conscience indicates the right course to take, we find we lack the will power to follow. As Paul said, 'My inner being delights in the law of God. But I see a different law in my body – a law which fights against the law my mind approves of. It makes me a prisoner to the law of sin which is in my body' (Rom. 7.22, 23).

And what about that third hall-mark of the divine image – man's *soul*? What effect does sin have upon that? The answer is that it destroys the communication between us and God. The line is cut. Man's sin (Gen. 3) was followed by his expulsion from the Garden of Eden and from the presence of God, and the gate was barred against his return. If physical death is one of the consequences of sin, an even more serious one is what is described in the Bible as spiritual death (Rom. 6.23), the complete alienation of man from God, and their separation from each other as though by some sort of iron curtain.

Cripples, prisoners and enemies – that is the picture of fallen man which is presented to us again and again in the Bible. Whenever man is described, it is always with one of these fatal flaws in evidence, and we stand in God's sight hopelessly devalued.

The Bible uses three words to describe our condition. The first is *'sin'* itself. This word implies a missing of the mark, or the failure to reach a required standard (Rom. 3.22, 23). It follows that to fail at all is to fail altogether (Jas. 2.10). For a service fault to be called at Wimbledon, the ball only has to miss the line by a fraction of an inch. It need not go ballooning into the Royal Box. Then there is the word *'Iniquity'* which means 'unequal' or 'out of line', and the thought this time is that of turning aside from the path which God has indicated (Isa. 53.6). The third word is *'transgression'* (or sometimes *'trespass'*) and it carries with it the idea of breaking a law or violating a frontier (1 John 3.4). Like the bowls player, man has failed in three ways. He has come short of the 'jack', he has twisted to one side, and he has gone too far.

The actual overt sins which man commits – murder, theft, adultery and so on – all stem from his initial act of disobedience. The Bible describes it as an infection passed from one generation to the next. Like some disgusting oil-slick, creeping into every corner and crevice of the coast line, it has touched us all with the pollution of its contaminating fingers. National, social, personal life are all infected; for 'there is none righteous, no, not one; there is none that understandeth, there is none that seeketh after God. They are all gone out of the way, they are together become unprofitable; there is none that doeth good, no, not one' (Rom. 3.10–12).

But happily that is not the final picture we are left with in the Bible, and we turn lastly to the *destiny of man*. What is God's ultimate desire and purpose for His creation? In a word, it is to restore what has been spoiled and damaged, and that we may be 'conformed to the image of His Son' (Rom. 8.29), and that He may be able to reproduce within us the likeness of Christ.

For the last hundred years or so, ever since Darwin, man has been far more concerned with and interested in his origin than his destiny. The question he is always asking is 'Where have I come from?' and not 'Why am I here?' and 'Where am I going?' And it is these questions that the Bible is so anxious to answer.

As we have already seen, man has been made for God, and he can only find a true meaning and purpose in life when that relationship has been restored, and what has been called 'the God-shaped cavity' has been filled. Man is his own worst enemy, and the reason why there is so much misery and unrest in the world today is not primarily political or economic, it is spiritual and moral; and it is only when man himself is re-united with his Maker that he will find that inner harmony which he craves, and the ability to live at peace with others.

Imagine that it were possible for you to leave this planet for two years, and that upon your return you found a completely different state of affairs in the world from the one which prevails today. Jew and Arab are living peaceably side by side. Black and white have discovered the secret of harmony and understanding. Management and labour have settled their differences. Peace reigns in Ireland, and there is a world-wide end to oppression, discrimination and the violation of human rights. To what would you attribute the cause of this Utopia? I would know the answer at once. It would not be due to some political alchemy or economic wizardry. I would know that in my absence there had been an outbreak of true spiritual religion of epidemic proportions, that men and women were acknowledging the sovereignty of God as never before, and making conformity to the will of Christ their sole ambition and criterion.

In one of his books on Europe, Bernard Newman tells the story of a small boy whose father was coaching him in geography. Finding a map of the world in a magazine, he cut it into small pieces jig-saw fashion and told his son to put it together again. The father was surprised when the boy returned a few minutes later with the map beautifully pasted together again. 'How did you do it so quickly?' he asked. 'Well,' said the boy, 'on the other side of the map I found a man, and when I put the man right, the world came right of its own accord.'

Whether such a state of affairs could ever exist, or is even expected in Scripture to do so, is very doubtful; but there have probably been a sufficient number of very limited and local examples of it to show us how the world's problems and ills could be solved 'at a stroke', to remind us of what it will be like when Christ Himself returns in triumph, and to encourage us to live in such a way that if others imitated us as we seek to imitate Christ, the world would be a great deal better and happier than it is at present.

5   The Cross

We have already had occasion to notice the astonishing emphasis which the New Testament places upon the death of Jesus, and marked the fact that it is the cross which has become the symbol of the Christian Faith. In this chapter we shall try to see the reason for this emphasis and for the significance of the death of Jesus, and to answer the question, 'Why the cross?'

The popular, superficial view, and the one which is probably most widely held amongst ordinary people, is that Jesus died as a martyr. The course of His life followed an all too familiar pattern. To His friends it was the old story of light clashing with darkness, good with evil and right with wrong: a common enough, though outstanding example of a man suffering at the hands of a wicked and envious clique of national leaders (Acts 2.22, 23).

His enemies of course saw it differently. To them He was a dangerous agitator who threatened the delicately balanced stance they were trying to adopt of co-existence with the Roman authorities. His death was regrettable, but a necessary price to pay if the whole nation was not to suffer (John 11.50). This is how historians like Josephus viewed the matter. This was the 'official explanation' for the record, and of course up to a point they were right. The death of Jesus was one more example of courageous martyrdom or political expediency, according to your particular standpoint.

But Christians, while admitting that this aspect of the death of Jesus cannot be ignored, find it quite impossible to accept it as an adequate explanation. Quite apart from the teaching of the New Testament on the subject, they point to the fact that Jesus need not have died: that, in His own words, He deliberately 'laid down His life' (John 10.17, 18). They demonstrate this by indicating that He could have prevented Judas from acting as he did; that He need not have gone to the one place, namely the Garden of Geth-

semane, where He knew His enemies would find Him; that
with the angelic hosts to help Him He could have resisted
arrest; and that when challenged to do so, He could have
come down from the cross. Furthermore, to those who are
still disposed to see nothing out of the ordinary in the death
of Jesus, they point to the resurrection, and argue from that
fact that the cross needs a theological as well as an historical
explanation.

But even among those who argue in this fashion there are
two sharply divergent views. First, there are those who take
what is called a subjective view of what happened. In their
view the death of Christ demonstrated the love of God in
such a dramatic and unmistakable way, that men and
women should be moved to repent and respond.

Others, while not denying what to them also is a very
real truth, feel that that explanation does not go far enough,
nor do adequate justice to the language of the New Testament. They take an objective view, and insist that the death
of Jesus actually achieved something which could not have
been achieved in any other way. In other words, He died
upon the cross not just to affect people's feelings, but to alter
facts.

Perhaps it can be illustrated in this way. Some little time
ago there was news in the papers and on television and radio
of a collision in Scotland between two aircraft. It was said
of one pilot that he did not bale out, as he could have done,
because he wanted to keep his machine airborne long enough
for it to avoid a densely populated area into which it would
otherwise have crashed. As a result of this he lost his life,
when a few seconds later the plane did finally crash, but in
a deserted part of the country.

Now reaction to that news would depend to some extent
upon where you happened to be living at the time. If, like
me, you were in no danger, because you were living in a
distant part of the country, you would have admired the
courage, devotion and self-sacrifice of the pilot, and you
were no doubt sufficiently inspired by his example to hope
that in similar circumstances you would act in the same
way. But if you happened to be living in that part of
Scotland which was threatened by the disaster, then the pilot
was very much more to you than an example. He was a
saviour. In Sussex, where I live, feelings were affected; but

in Scotland, where the danger lay, facts were altered. And it is because of what Jesus did upon the cross that His death is of such significance.

Most people's deaths pass unnoticed, so far as the general public is concerned. They are of no great significance. The world pauses for a moment, and then goes on exactly as before. But now and then someone's death affects the lives of other people in a deep and radical way, and may even alter the whole course of history: a fortune changes hands, a nation finds itself at war, a new dictator emerges. And that is the way in which the New Testament looks at the death of Jesus. Things were never the same again, because His death did not simply change our attitude towards God, but His attitude towards us. In what way did it do this?

The word normally used to describe what happened upon the cross is 'atonement'. It means the bringing together or the setting 'at one' two people who have fallen out with each other. Man, through his sin, was estranged from God, and the death of Jesus effected an 'at-one-moment'.

When we start to study the New Testament on this subject, we find that there are what might be called four 'categories of thought'. To some extent they overlap and inter-twine, and it would be a mistake to make the divisions between them too sharp, but with that qualification they provide perhaps the most helpful way of examining and understanding the doctrine of the atonement. We might label them the financial, the personal, the moral and the legal.

There are several passages in the New Testament which emphasize the first, and in the early centuries of Christian history it was probably the most popular aspect of this truth. In brief it amounts to this: that man is a prisoner, taken captive by sin, and a price has to be paid for his redemption.

It used to be necessary to go back to the days of Richard Coeur de Lion to find an example of a ransom, but now unfortunately it is all too common for men and women to be kidnapped by bandits and held up for ransom. Every effort is then made to secure their release by raising the money demanded.

So it was that Jesus referred to Himself as 'the ransom' (Mark 10.45) which had to be paid if we were to be redeemed from sin. 'There was no other good enough to pay

the price of sin', for as Peter reminds us, we 'were not
redeemed with corruptible things like silver and gold . . . but
with the precious blood of Christ' (1 Pet. 1.18, 19). People
have been tempted to try to push this analogy too far, and
to ask to whom the ransom was paid. The logical answer
would of course have to be 'the devil', but that is an
unthinkable absurdity, and we are reminded that metaphors
and parables such as this one are not meant to apply in every
detail, and that we are to be content with the broad outline
of the lesson taught. It is perhaps for this reason that this
particular metaphor does not stand alone, but is comple-
mented by others in order to give us a fuller understanding
of what took place upon the cross.

And so we pass to the second line of thought – what I
have called the personal aspect of the atonement. Sometimes
we read of a man who has been grossly slandered or libelled,
his honour or integrity have been impugned, and he goes to
court to seek what is called 'satisfaction'. If he is a very
important person, and the libel particularly offensive, then
of course the damages can be very great; for we must
remember that the gravity of an offence of this sort is to
some extent measured by the dignity of the person against
whom it is committed; and if in the case of God the dignity
is immeasurable, then so is the offence.

But it often happens in some such civil case that there is
a settlement out of court. The plaintiff agrees to drop proceedings against the man who has wronged him on account
of a sum of money paid to him by way of reparation. In our
case too, God has agreed, as it were, to settle out of court;
but He is only able to do so, because Jesus in His great love
has 'made . . . a full, perfect and sufficient sacrifice, oblation,
and *satisfaction*, for the sins of the whole world'. In this way
God is propitiated (1 John 2.1, 2) or satisfied, His honour
is vindicated, and 'proceedings' are dropped. This personal
aspect of the atonement introduces us to a whole range of
words like 'pardon', 'reconciliation' (2 Cor. 5.19; Col. 1.20)
and 'forgiveness' (Eph. 1.7). They all convey the idea of a
friendly relationship which has been broken by our sin, and
then restored through the death of Christ.

The next dimension of the atonement which we must look
at is the moral one. This relates to the defilement of sin. It
regards us as moral lepers, isolated from God, unfit for His

presence, and in need of cleansing if we are to be received by Him. It was perhaps this aspect of the atonement which appealed particularly to Jewish minds, because for centuries they had been taught that the only way into the holiest place, the presence of God Himself, was through the sacrifice of some animal and the shedding of its blood. It corresponded therefore with all that they had been taught in the Old Testament when they learned that they could only 'enter the holiest by the blood of Jesus, by a new and living way which He has consecrated for us, through the veil, that is to say, His flesh' (Heb. 10.19, 20); and it was this that John the Baptist had in mind when pointing to Jesus he said, 'Behold, the Lamb of God who bears away the sin of the world' (John 1.29).

No ordinary person can make his way unbidden into the presence of the Queen, for we have no automatic right of access; but if we happened to be friendly with, or even related to a member of the Royal Family, it would be a very different matter. We would be accepted for the sake of that royal person. So it is that we are disqualified from entering the presence of God until Jesus Christ, so to speak, takes us by the hand and introduces us on the grounds of what He has done for us upon the cross. We are then, as Paul puts it, 'accepted in the beloved' (Eph. 1.6).

And so we come to the last of these four aspects or dimensions of the atonement – to the one I have referred to as 'legal'. The key word this time is not Redemption, or Forgiveness, or Cleansing, but Justification. This was a truth which lay concealed for many centuries, covered with the dust of ignorance and distortion, until it was restored with such dramatic effect to the prominence it deserved by Martin Luther in the sixteenth century.

It introduces us to the most serious aspect of sin, and therefore to the deepest meaning of the cross; for as we saw in an earlier chapter, sin not only spoils our lives and imprisons us, but it alienates us from God (Col. 1.21). It is the transgression of His laws, and so exposes us to His judgement and punishment. 'The wages of sin is death' (Rom. 6.23), which means expulsion from the presence of God now and for ever.

When Jesus died upon the cross, He accepted the judgement of God upon sin, and bore the penalty in our place. He

was in fact our substitute. It is impossible to find or invent a
human analogy to cover this situation, because no reasonable
legal system would allow an innocent victim to be substi-
tuted for a guilty person. Perhaps the nearest we can get to
it is to think of Jesus as the Judge, paying the fine which
the law required, because we, the guilty and convicted party,
were unable to meet it ourselves. But the reasonableness, or
what Paul calls the 'wisdom' of the cross (1 Cor. 1.23, 24),
lies in the fact that the Godhead is so constituted that the
Law Giver, the Judge, the Victim of the offence and the
innocent Substitute were all one and the same Person.

It was while He hung there in the darkness that there was
torn from the lips of Jesus that awful cry of dereliction, as
He 'was made sin for us' (2 Cor. 5.20) : 'My God, My God,
why hast Thou forsaken Me?' (Matt. 27.46). What He
suffered physically must have been fearful enough, but it
was as nothing compared with that deeper inner anguish as
His soul was made an offering for sin (Isa. 53.10), and the
light of God's presence was extinguished. Our banishment
from God's presence would have been measured in length.
His was measured in depth. It has been well expressed in
words which Elizabeth Barrett Browning wrote, and which
appear on the grave of William Cowper:

> Yet once Immanuel's orphan cry His universe
>   hath shaken,
> It went up single, echoless, My God I am
>   forsaken;
> It went up from the holy lips amid a lost
>   creation,
> That of the lost no sons should use those words
>   of desolation.

We have examined the atonement under four separate
heads, and we have done so deliberately, but it must be
repeated that while the Bible lends itself to this sort of
treatment, it does not divide its doctrines into neat, water-
tight compartments. There is a great deal of over-lapping
and inter-locking. You can categorize the ingredients which
go to compose a cake, but that is not the way it is finally
appreciated and enjoyed. It is enjoyed as a whole, as an
entity. While therefore this analysis may have proved help-

ful, it would be a mistake to press it too far, or to allow it to obscure the over-all wonder of the cross of Christ. The atonement is far greater than the sum of its parts, and we can lose something of that wonder if we try to dissect it too precisely.

Writing to the Galatians, Paul said, 'God forbid that I should glory, save in the cross of our Lord Jesus Christ' (Gal. 6.14). Humanly speaking, Paul had much to boast about. He combined within himself all the finest attributes of those three races of the ancient world – the Jews, the Greeks and the Romans. He was a man of great moral integrity and rectitude; of immense intellectual stature; and possessing extraordinary resources of courage and physical endurance. And yet when he compared these things with the cross, they counted for precisely nothing.

There was nothing attractive about the cross. As we have already seen, it disfigured society for about a thousand years, and modern forms of execution such as the gallows and even the gas chamber seem almost civilized by comparison. But to Paul, and indeed to every Christian ever since, it has been the greatest thing in the world, because it is there that they have seen the wisdom of God, the love of God and the power of God.

That is not how it appeared to Paul's contemporaries. To the Greeks the whole idea was contemptible foolishness, a sort of sick joke. To the Jews it was the very opposite of love, indeed an outrageous scandal that God could allow His Messiah to suffer such an appalling fate. While to the Romans, it was the ultimate demonstration of weakness and defeat.

But how differently it appears to us! It is there that we see the wisdom of God, as He solved the age-old problem of man's re-entry into the atmosphere of His presence. It is there that we see the love of God, as He put this amazing rescue operation into effect. It is there too, that we see the power of God, when we think of the dynamic influence of the cross, and of the millions who have found forgiveness and life at its foot (1 Cor. 1.17–25).

But at this point two questions arise. First, it is sometimes asked how the death of one person, nearly two thousand years ago can atone for the sins of the whole world, and especially for the sins of people who at that time had never lived. The answer lies in the nature and character of the person who died; for we must remember that it was not only what Jesus did upon the cross that counted for so much, but who He was. He was not just a very great teacher and prophet, but the eternal Son of God Himself. He was not just a very good man, He was completely without sin. And it is these two facts, His divinity and His sinlessness, which make His death of such eternal and infinite value and importance to mankind.

The second question is this: Is there nothing that we can do to atone for our own sin? After all, these are the days of 'do-it-yourself'. We are constantly reminded that we live in a meritocracy, where the prizes go to the swift and the strong. The idea of inheriting wealth or receiving something for nothing is regarded in some quarters as undesirable and even abhorrent. Why therefore can we not earn our own salvation?

The first answer must surely be that such an arrangement would be grossly unfair, because so many are born into a squalid environment or a bad home where there is no moral encouragement or example; and then there are those who start life with the grave disadvantage of some inherited liability, or a miserable perversion, mental instability or physical defect. For everyone to start level, and to enjoy an equal chance of reaching heaven under their own steam, some incredibly complicated system of handicapping would have to be invented, with points deducted from those who began life with great natural advantages and added to those who did not.

A second reason is that given by Paul himself (Eph. 2.8–10). This arrangement, he says, would never do, because it would lead to boasting and pride. Just imagine what heaven would be like if we all owed our presence there to our own good deeds – a veritable 'prig-sty'! No! Heaven will be more like a kind of Club in which there are only 'honorary members'. We shall be there, not because we deserve to be, having paid our way and earned our passage, but because we have been invited *honoris causa*, the 'honour', of course, being not ours, but Christ's. The door into heaven is at the foot of the cross, and not at the top of the ladder.

The third reason is quite simply this: We can't afford the subscription. It is too great. The pass mark is too high. As the hymn puts it, 'Not the labour of my hands can fulfil Thy laws demand . . . all for sin could not atone, Thou must save and Thou alone'. Isaiah in one place describes our righteousness as 'filthy rags' (Isa. 64.6). Most of us would be prepared to have our sins described in that way, but Isaiah is speaking of our righteousness, our very best deeds: our Sunday suit, not our oldest gardening clothes. We are like someone who has to decline an invitation to an important party or reception because he has nothing suitable to wear.

This point was well illustrated in a story Jesus told about a wedding reception. Those invited were provided, on arrival, with a special robe which, besides reflecting the glory and wealth of the host, also served to eliminate any sense of shame or pride (as the case might be) on the part of the guests. But the party had a gate-crasher. We are not told what he was wearing, but he refused the offer of the wedding gown, presumably because he thought his own tailor-made suit altogether superior. He was given very short shrift, and was quickly shown the door, expelled by his own ingratitude and pride.

We too can only be accepted by God if we discard what we are wearing, whether we realize that it is 'too bad', or think it may be 'good enough', and receive the robe of Christ's righteousness. It is only when we are clothed in that way that we can be admitted into God's presence (Isa. 61.10).

One of our chief problems is that we are so apt to compare ourselves with each other, and we usually manage to think of people with whom we compare rather favourably. But God compares us with the standard which Jesus set, and to fall short of that is to fail completely. There is no human detergent which can produce the same dazzling whiteness as the snow, and there is nothing we can do which will fit us for the presence of God. We are like Lady Macbeth, contemplating her guilt: 'All the perfumes of Arabia will not sweeten this little hand.' Nothing can do that – 'nothing but the blood of Jesus.'

We must remember too that good deeds in the future cannot undo the past. Good resolutions won't mend broken laws; and even if from now on we could live the perfect life, there would still be the past failures for which we would have to account and for which we would be responsible.

Finally, and perhaps almost too obviously, there is no point in trying to earn what Christ is waiting and wanting to offer us as a gift. Why bother to row, if the boat you are in is equipped with an engine? Why go on batting when the match has already been won? Why offer to pay for the present which someone has already bought for you? We shall want to show our gratitude, of course, by the way we live; but we show it first by the way we take, humbly and thankfully, what God is offering to us (Psa. 116.12, 13).

Almost the last words which Jesus uttered upon the cross took the form of a shout of triumph – 'It is finished' (John 19.30). He meant that He had settled the debt, paid the ransom and borne the penalty. Now He offers the benefits of His death and passion as a free gift to all who will believe.

> All is finished, and nothing remains
> But man's acceptance of Calvary's gains.

6 Commitment

The New Testament distinguishes between two kinds of faith. There is intellectual assent and there is personal commitment; or, as it has sometimes been described, there is 'believing about' and 'believing in'. In other words, it is perfectly possible to be an orthodox believer without being a true Christian. The Devil himself presumably falls into this category (Jas. 2.19). No one understands or believes the facts of Christianity more firmly than he; but his is hardly the kind of faith which is likely to lead to any sort of Christian commitment.

The difference between these two kinds of faith may be simply illustrated as follows. Imagine two men waiting at a bus stop. They are both equally convinced that the bus will come, and that it is going in the direction they want. The time-table tells them so. Their own observation on previous occasions confirms the fact; while if they wanted further re-assurance, they have only to ask the other would-be passengers standing by. Eventually the bus arrives, but while the first man gets on to it, his companion, who has come to see him off, waves good-bye and turns away. Both men exhibited faith, but only the first man actually committed himself to the bus.

It is for this reason that we often find the Greek word for 'believing' or 'having faith' followed by the preposition *eis* or *en,* suggesting motion into or upon; and it is this step of faith which the Bible tells us will bring a person from darkness to light, and from condemnation to salvation (John 3.16; 5.24).

This act of faith is described in several ways in the Bible. For example, we read of people 'coming to Christ' (Matt. 11.28. John 6.37), or 'following Him' (John 1.37), 'trusting' (Eph. 1.12) and 'receiving' Him (John 1.12. Rev. 3.20). The actual metaphor is of course of less importance than the fact it represents. What matters when we need the services of a doctor is not whether he comes to us or we go to him in his surgery, but the personal encounter which brings us both together; and so it is with our relationship with Christ.

But is such a step really necessary? The Bible and all experience tell us that it is. We cannot drift into the Kingdom of God, we must enter it by a deliberate and definite act of will. It is one thing to be a vague supporter of a football club or political party, but quite another to be a fully paid-up and committed member.

At one stage in his great and distinguished career, Sir Winston Churchill used to describe his attitude towards the Christian Church as that of a 'flying buttress', because, he said, he supported it from without. There are many like that. They feel that the Church, as an institution is something to be preserved at almost any cost, and that somehow the world without Christianity would be vastly worse off. But that is as far as they go. Their attachment stops short of any kind of personal commitment. Their benevolent neutrality is not to be despised. Indeed, we should be grateful for it. But if such people were closely questioned, they would probably have to admit that in any meaningful sense they were not Christians at all.

Christians are often asked whether they believe in sudden conversion, or whether the sort of experience I have been describing is a gradual process. It is true that some have a far more dramatic experience than others. Some are awoken with all the unexpected suddenness of an alarm clock, while others wake up more slowly, as the sun begins to creep round the curtains. On the Damascus road, the light 'flashed' upon Saul of Tarsus; but on the road to Emmaus (Luke 24) it 'dawned' upon Cleopas and his companion.

But of course every conversion, if we could analyze it, is both gradual and sudden. The approach is gradual, but the action is sudden. This is so with every decision we make, whether crossing a frontier, entering a room, signing a cheque or proposing marriage. It may take weeks or even months of careful thought before we reach the decisive point, but the final step is a matter of moments. We are told, for example, that Abraham Lincoln spent the whole of one night pacing up and down in his room before he could bring himself to put his name to some fateful document which required his signature – an act which would have taken him barely five seconds.

The metaphor which Jesus used to describe conversion was that of a new birth (John 3.5). Not only does this introduce us to a deep theological understanding of what takes place when we come to Christ (and we shall return to this later), but it also illustrates perfectly the relationship between the gradual and the immediate: between the process and the crisis. The process, as we know, takes months; but the crisis of actual birth is immediate, so that we do not talk about a 'birth-month', or even a 'birth-week', but always a 'birthday'.

It is at this point that we must consider certain questions and difficulties which often arise in the minds of those who, under the influence of the Holy Spirit, as Christians believe, are seriously considering this act of personal commitment to Christ. The first is this: 'What exactly do I have to do?'

We must of course assume that the questioner has reached this culminating point, and is about to 'cross the frontier', only after he has passed certain important milestones on the way. He has seen clearly that he is a sinner in need of forgiveness, and that God must judge and punish that sin (Rom. 3.22, 23, 6.23). He has seen, secondly, that Christ has died upon the cross to deal with those sins, and by bearing the penalty of them in his place, He is able to blot them out for ever (John 3.16; Isa. 53.6; 1 Pet. 2.24, 3.18). And finally he has seen that to follow Christ sincerely will mean a complete break with past sin (Isa. 55.7) and a willingness to be known as one of His disciples (Luke 9.23). The question he is asking therefore has its roots in a long process of thought, involving mind, conscience and heart.

It is quite often the case that he needs to be disabused of certain ideas. It is not a question of turning over a new leaf, or making some good resolutions about going to church and prayer and so on. These things are important, but they do not constitute conversion, they follow it.

To any who ask this question, the answer must surely be that they should make up a simple prayer in their own words to Christ, telling Him that they are sorry for their sins, thanking Him for His death for them upon the cross, and then inviting Him into their lives, rather as they might ask a friend who had called to enter their house (Rev. 3.20).

But there is a second question which occurs to some

people, and it is this: 'Isn't it all too simple? How can so
much turn upon so little? Does my eternal salvation really
depend upon a single act of my own freewill?'

The answer must be that very often an enormous issue
may turn on a very small axis, just as small keys can open
large doors, and small rudders determine the course of
great ships. It is the simplest thing in the world to sign one's
name, and is probably a thing many of us do several times
a day. But if that signature is going to involve some business
contract running into millions of pounds, or authorize an
order affecting the lives of countless people, then it is only
going to be made after long and earnest thought, and with
a clear understanding of all that is involved. Simplicity in
itself is no criterion of importance. It is a very simple thing
to turn to Christ, but the causes of that step and its consequences can be of enormous significance for life and for
eternity. Because a thing is simple, it does not follow that it
is therefore easy.

But think what it would be like if this act of commitment
were not a simple one. Suppose God required us to solve
some abstruse theological cross-word puzzle! Who then
would be saved? Or suppose we were only allowed into the
Kingdom of God if we could solve some of the deep mysteries
of life, such as the problem of suffering or evil! How many
of us would win a place? We are saved by faith and not by
works, or even by understanding (Eph. 2.8–10). Indeed, we
shall never reach a full understanding in this life. Our motto
must be, *Credo ut intellagam* – 'I believe so that I may
understand', and not vice versa. A man's reach will always
exceed his grasp, and there will be things which we must
touch by faith but which we shall never apprehend with our
mind.

The third question is this: 'How can I be sure that Christ
has responded to my prayer and come into my life?' People
are sometimes disappointed because they do not experience
a sudden access of joyful feelings, and they begin to doubt
whether anything has happened at all. This makes them
wonder whether they have believed hard enough, or whether
their faith was of the right sort. What they need to remember is that God is far more ready to hear than we are to
pray. Christ does not need to be persuaded to come into our
lives. He is waiting and willing to do so, and will respond

to the first indication on our part that we want Him. The man who cried, 'Lord, I believe, help Thou mine unbelief' (Mark 9.24) was just as richly rewarded as the woman to whom Jesus said, 'O woman, great is your faith' (Matt. 15.28). It is not how I believe that saves me, but whom I believe. You don't have to persuade the wind to fill the sail, you only have to hold the sail up.

So the first answer to this question is that we must simply take Christ at His word. He has promised that He will come into our lives, that He will receive us, and we can rely upon Him to keep His promise. But it won't be very long before we begin to have what Paul calls the 'witness of the Spirit' within ourselves (Rom. 8.16). In other words, Christ cannot dwell within us without making a noticeable difference. We shall find, for example, that we now want to overcome the temptations which previously, perhaps, we were quite content to give in to. We shall find that the Bible and prayer take on a new meaning and significance in our lives. We shall find that we start to enjoy the company of other Christians, even those with whom, apart from our new-found faith, we seem to have little in common. We shall find that in some strange and inexplicable way life has somehow acquired a new purpose, a new sense of direction, in fact a new dimension. We shall find that even the world itself will take on a new complexion and a new beauty which 'Christ-less eyes have never seen'. As John Masefield puts it in 'The Everlasting Mercy'

> The station brook to my new eyes
> Was babbling out of paradise.

This is what Paul meant when he said, 'If any man be in Christ, he is a new creation [a new being]. Old things have passed away, behold all things are become new' (2 Cor. 5.17).

And so assurance in this matter depends upon two things: the evidence of God's Word and the experience of our own lives. We might compare our situation to that of someone who for some reason is trying to prove his identity. How can he be sure that he is who he thinks he is? First, there is his birth certificate, a document which makes it perfectly clear that he belongs to his parents. This is his final authority. But for practical purposes he relies upon more experimental evidence. There is the family likeness, the family ties, the family affections. Together these two things prove to him that he is who he is, and remove any lingering doubts concerning his identity.

The next question that bothers some people is this: 'How can I keep it up?' They don't want to embark on something which they will not find themselves able to continue to the end. They feel like a man who inherits a country estate without the means to maintain it. He has to give it up, because he can't keep it up. The answer is that Christ puts at our disposal, as it were, the 'income' we need, and that as we look to Him and wait upon Him in prayer and Bible reading, and use the other means of grace which He has provided, we shall find that 'as our days, so shall our strength be' (Deut. 33.25).

'But what if we do fall? Will Christ leave me again?' The very metaphor of the new birth which we have been studying really answers that question. We may become prodigal sons, but once we are born into God's family, we are His children for ever, and He will never cast us out (John 6.37).

And again, as we have seen, we are 'a new creation'. We are all familiar with the difference between a physical and a chemical change. The first is reversible (ice into water), but the second is not; for if iron filings and sulphur are heated together then a new substance (ferrous sulphide) emerges. And when we become Christians, it is a change of the second sort and not the first sort that takes place. 'A new creation', 'a Christian' is brought into existence, and nothing can reverse that fact.

If we do fall, as we are bound to do from time to time, we must pick ourselves up, ask Christ to forgive us, see if we can find out where we went wrong, and determine in His strength not to be defeated in the same way again. But the Christian life is not like one of those games where one false move sends you back to the beginning, to start all over again. It is more like chess, where even in defeat, you can never lose your King.

But we must remember that this crisis of conversion or personal commitment to Christ is not only preceded by a process it is also followed by one – the process of growth into Christian maturity and likeness to Christ. Let us imagine a

Frenchman who wants to become a naturalized Englishman. No doubt various references are checked and papers signed, and then, perhaps after many months, on a given day, he finds himself an Englishman.

But while that final step ended one process it began another, because it may be many months and even years before English idioms, habits and customs become second nature to him, and he is recognized as unmistakably English; indeed, to the very end of his life there will almost certainly linger the vestigial remains of his old, French nature, quiescent perhaps, and even dormant, but never wholly extinct.

It is the difference between a man's 'status' and his 'state'. His status may change overnight, but his state only after a long period of conditioning. Put theologically, we say that Justification is a crisis and Sanctification is a process. In the New Testament the word 'Justification' is never used in its derivative, but always in its popular sense: not to 'make righteous', but to 'reckon righteous'; the word 'Sanctification' being used to describe the process by which we are 'made righteous'. 'Transferred' (Col. 1.13), we must now be 'transformed' (Rom. 12.2).

In other words, it is the Christian's duty to become what he is. He is a Christian, but he must become Christ-like. He is a Saint, but he must become Saintly. He is justified (reckoned righteous) and he must become sanctified (made righteous). But to the very end of his life there will remain traces, and very often more than just traces, of that old sinful nature which dominated his life before his conversion, and which Paul refers to in many places as 'the flesh'. Like the naturalized Englishman, we shall never be able completely to disguise our origins. The old nature will never be wholly eradicated, and there will be times when some word, thought or action will betray to ourselves and to others that we were once citizens of the kingdom of darkness.

This process of sanctification will depend upon our doing two things – 'Mortify' and 'Fortify'. The old nature (the 'French' part of us) must steadily be put to death (Col. 3.5; Rom. 8.13) and the new nature cultivated and encouraged (Col. 3.2, 12). In the Baptismal Service in the 1662 Prayer Book it is put in this quaint but impressive way. Referring to the newly baptized person we are asked to pray that 'all carnal affections may die in him, and all things belonging to the Spirit may live and grow in him'.

It is obvious that if the naturalized Englishman wants to 'become what he is', English in character as well as in name, then he will not be for ever dashing off to France, or hankering after French literature, companionship and food. He will 'mortify' that side of his nature, and do all he can to 'fortify' the tastes, attitudes and habits of an Englishman.

And so it should be with the Christian. He will do as little as possible to pander to the tastes and inclinations of 'the flesh', ignoring its pleas and refusing to satisfy its appetites. At the same time he will do all he can to nourish and cultivate the life of 'the Spirit'. He will enjoy the companionship of other Christians, the language of prayer will become his, while for literature he will find nothing to compare with the Bible.

7   The Bible

Even the most radical and violent critics find themselves compelled to admit that there is something about the Bible which is unique, and which sets it apart from every other book. Indeed, the very hostility it provokes and the lengths to which governments have been prepared to go to stamp it out and to prevent its distribution, are indicative of the same thing.

It has become a truism to say that it is the most popular book in the world, but its continuous and enormous sales, the range of its translations into other languages and dialects, and its persistence in the teeth of repeated attempts to eradicate it – all these facts show what an immense and powerful hold it has had upon the minds of people all down the years.

And its influence upon countries like our own, where for centuries it has enjoyed freedom, is profound. It has helped to shape our laws, it has coloured our literature and seeped into our conversation and speech. Attempts by some of the newer English versions to replace phrases like 'den of thieves,' 'the fatted calf' and 'the salt of the earth' have been doomed to failure, simply because the older phrases have rooted themselves so firmly in the structure of our language, and become part of the English idiom.

But those who expose their hearts and minds to the teaching of the Bible would go a good deal further than this. They find that it is not only the most popular book in the world, but also the most powerful. They would describe the Bible as alive, as a living book, because wherever it is received it seems to fertilize the mind in such a way that something new is actually created. We have all read books which have excited and entertained us, but the Bible does more, for it actually transforms us. As Peter puts it in his letter, 'You have been born anew . . . through the living and abiding word of God' (1 Pet. 1.23). It is as though by planting a book about roses in the soil of your garden you could literally grow the very flowers which it describes and depicts.

Individuals, homes, communities and even countries have been changed for the better by the reading of this book. Speaking many years ago at a meeting of the British and Foreign Bible Society, Stanley Baldwin, at that time Prime Minister of Great Britain said this: 'The Bible is high explosive. But it works in strange ways, and no living man can tell or know how that book, in its journey through the world, has startled the individual soul in ten thousand different places into a new life, a new world, a new belief, a new conception, and a new faith.'

It was another Prime Minister, Ramsay Macdonald, whose government negotiated the purchase of the famous Codex Sinaiticus from Soviet Russia by the trustees of the British Museum. The price paid was £100,000, which was a lot of money in 1933, when you could post a letter for just over ½p and the London *Times* was twenty times cheaper than it is today. There was something symbolic in this trans- action: that the book which was officially rejected in Russia should find a home in the heart of London; and perhaps the freedom and tolerance still enjoyed in this country are not unconnected with the fact that we are prepared to pay that sort of price for a copy of the Bible.

However that may be, it is a fact that for millions of people the Bible is not only the most popular and the most powerful book in the world, but also the most precious, and the one from which they would least want to be parted. Their feeling about it is well expressed at a dramatic moment in the Coronation Service when the Sovereign is presented with a copy of the Bible which is handed to her with these words: 'We present you with this Book, the most valuable thing that this world affords. Here is wisdom; this is the royal Law; these are the lively oracles of God.'

What accounts for the astonishing hold which the Bible has on the hearts and minds of people all over the world? Why in the Radio Programme 'Desert Island Discs' is it almost the only book which the 'Castaway' need not take with him to his exile because it is already there? The first answer to these questions lies in the appeal of the Bible. Of course all books have some sort of appeal, but it is usually a fairly limited one which is one reason why there have to be so many books. Go into any public library, and you will see people scattered around looking for books in different sections – biography, fiction, science, sport, travel and so on. What appeals to one person holds no attraction for another, and vice versa.

But the remarkable, indeed the unique thing about the Bible is the universal nature of its appeal. There is no other book like it in this respect. People whose tastes in other forms of literature are widely apart, find themselves united in their love for the Bible, and in the pleasure they derive from reading it. It is 'the book of the people'; and young and old, rich and poor, wise and simple, black and white, whatever the differences may be in their culture and background, find inspiration and comfort in its pages.

The reason for this astonishing appeal is not hard to find. The Bible speaks to the whole man. There is no mood, no experience, no circumstances and no state of mind which it fails to match with a message of comfort, encouragement or rebuke. It has something to say to the tempted, the disappointed, the perplexed, the suffering and the sorrowful.

And it speaks to us at every level. If we think of man as composed of mind, heart, conscience and will, then the Bible will, if we allow it to do so, speak to each in turn. It will illumine the mind, warm the heart, stir the conscience and strengthen the will. We cannot get out of range of its promises, its commands, its encouragements and its warnings.

There are those who complain that the Bible is too difficult or too dull, and they give that as an excuse for not exploring its depths. It is quite true that there are parts of it which are best understood with the help of a commentary or explanatory notes. It is also true that for those who have never really started out upon the Christian life it is dull and uninteresting. It is like a map which they are studying in a geography text-book compared with one they are examining for pleasure, because it describes the country they have begun to explore.

But there is I think another reason why many people do not read the Bible. They find it too disturbing. It is indeed 'high explosive'. Its demands are exacting, its standards uncomfortably high and its challenge inescapable. This is why some react to it as King Jehoiakim did. He sat one day in his 'winter house' listening as his secretary read to him from the Scriptures. But after hearing three or four pages, we are told that he had had enough, and slashing the scroll with his knife, he threw it into the fire that was burning in front of him on the hearth (Jer. 36.20–23).

But if we are scanning a library shelf for a book, or wondering how best to spend a token, we want to find out a little more than the class of person to whom the book will appeal. We want to know its aim. What is it trying to do? Is it seeking to amuse me, excite me, inform me, or what? And we are justified in putting that question to the Bible. What exactly is it trying to do?

The answer that Christians have always given to that question is that in the pages of the Bible we have a special revelation of the mind and will and character of God Himself. We speak of a 'special revelation', because in the world of nature we have a 'general revelation', where the everlasting power and wisdom of God may be clearly seen (Rom. 1.20). But alongside this general revelation is another type which we call 'special', because it is adapted to man, not so much as man, but as a sinner; and this revelation is provided for us, not in the works of nature, but in the words of the Bible. These two species of revelation, general and special, or, as they are sometimes called, natural and supernatural, are brought together for us in one memorable passage in the psalms: 'The heavens declare the glory of God . . . the law of the Lord is perfect, restoring the soul' (Psa. 19.1–7).

The supernatural revelation of God's grace was progressive. It was granted first to individuals, and then in succession to a family, a tribe and a nation; until, with the coming of Christ, it was made available to the whole world. And not only was this revelation progressive in terms of width, but also in depth, as we trace the story of man's redemption from its earliest hints and faintest outlines to its glorious fulfilment in Christ.

This supernatural revelation of God took place in what appear to be three distinct ways. It would be an oversimplification to say that they correspond exactly to the patriarchal, the prophetic and the apostolic phases of Biblical history, but there is a discernible relationship of this sort. In the early days it was chiefly by manifestation that God made Himself known, through symbols and theophanies: the burning bush, the pillars of cloud, and by visitations of angels and men.

The second phase, overlapping and inter-locking with the

others, was dictation. 'Behold, I have put my words in your mouth' (Jer. 1.9; Isa. 51.16); 'Son of man . . . Go and speak with my words to them' (Ezek. 3.4). The word 'prophet' throughout Scripture means 'spokesman', almost 'the mouth of God'. Today when we are told that a 'Home Office' or 'Foreign Office Spokesman' has made some pronouncement, we know that it bears the official imprimatur of the Government. So it was with the prophets of old. We do not know, nor does it greatly matter, what particular processes were used to accomplish this form of dictation. It is perhaps as aptly described as anywhere in the words of the Lord to Moses, 'the reluctant spokesman', when He said, 'I will be with your mouth and teach you what you shall say' (Ex. 4.12).

The third phase might be described as suggestion. In this case the revelation of God's truth is achieved through the action of human powers in the form of historical research, logical reasoning or ethical thought, not acting by themselves, but under the prevailing assistance, guidance and control of the Holy Spirit. The idea is not that the Holy Spirit is standing beside the writers, making good any deficiencies in their work, or supplementing their own human thought, but rather that He is operating within them (2 Pet. 1.21).

Perhaps we can illustrate the difference between these two modes of revelation – dictation and suggestion – in this way. Imagine a man who has two secretaries. To the first he dictates his letters, word for word, and she faithfully reproduces what he has expressed. The second is different. She so knows the mind of her employer, we will suppose, and is so imbued with his spirit, that dictation is unnecessary. Unconsciously, perhaps, but as faithfully as her colleague, she reproduces her employer's thought. 'She knows his mind', as we say – which is only another way of expressing what Paul said when he wrote, 'We have the mind of Christ' (1 Cor. 2.16). To make the analogy fit, of course, we have to imagine a degree of confluence which could never be achieved in any human relationship, and which protects the text from actual error; but the illustration will serve to express the idea, and to indicate the difference between dictation and direction as it applies to God's methods of revelation in the Bible.

This leads us on quite naturally to the third feature we look for in a book we are thinking of buying or borrowing, namely its authority for, unless the work is one of purely imaginative fiction, we want to be sure that we are being told the truth. In the case of the Bible it follows as a matter of course that if the writers are performing their task at the dictation or under the direction of God, then the results must have the stamp of divine authority.

We must distinguish at this point between what might be called the seat of authority and its source. Perhaps we can illustrate it in this way. In a democracy, like our own, the source of authority lies with the people. It is they who elect or reject the government. But the seat of authority is parliament; for it is in parliament that the people deposit and express their authority.

In the same way, the ultimate fountain and source of authority in matters of faith and conduct must and can only be Almighty God Himself. 'There is no authority except from God' (Rom. 13.1), for 'power belongs to God' (Psa. 62.11). But for practical purposes God has deposited this authority in Scripture. He has provided us with what might be called 'a written constitution'.

To have made Scripture the seat of authority in this way is eminently reasonable. Again and again when we want something officially recorded or authoritatively expressed, we say, 'put it in writing'. A person's Will is a good example of how we do this in practice. What is written becomes at once universally and permanently available, and though its precise interpretation must be a matter for the experts to decide, there is little or no dispute as to what is actually written, and what it is that they are trying to interpret.

Of course it goes without saying that the actual writing of Scripture was not done by God Himself. This task was performed by a host of different people over many centuries. But we may fairly speak of God as the 'Author' of Scripture. Normally, we know, the author and the writer of a book are one and the same person, but not always, and not necessarily so. We can take an analogy from the relationship which exists between Architect and Builder. Sir Christopher Wren's name, for example, is for ever associated with St Paul's Cathedral. He was the architect, but it is unlikely that he ever wielded a tool or handled a stone. The actual building was done by a host of unnamed and long-forgotten stone masons, joiners and carvers at his dictation and under his direction. He inspired what they did.

This introduces us to a very important word concerning Scripture, namely Inspiration. It is one which the Bible uses of itself when it says that 'all Scripture is given by inspiration of God' (2 Tim. 3.16) — or literally, 'all Scripture is God-breathed'. Sometimes we hear people speaking of 'an inspired leak', and we know that a rumour, normally to be accepted with caution and even suspicion, is on this occasion emanating from an authoritative source, and is to be trusted. This is what the Bible is claiming for itself — that 'holy men spoke as they were moved (literally, "borne", as the wind might carry you along) by the Holy Spirit' (2 Pet. 1.21).

The word as used in the Bible means 'out-breathed' rather than 'in-breathed'. It conveys the idea of God having breathed out Scripture rather than having breathed His authority into Scripture already written. That is why Scripture is often referred to as 'the word of God' or 'God's word', even though it was spoken through men's lips or written with their pens. And that is why also we find our-selves obliged to use the phrase 'verbal inspiration' when describing the Bible, because it is the words themselves, and not just the ideas which they express, which are God-breathed. At the same time we must not suppose that God in some way over-ruled the writers' personality, background, education or style. It was not that He conditioned people to write what He wanted, but rather that He formed and chose people who would spontaneously write in that way.

We must now look at a second aspect of authority which has already been hinted at, and that is Interpretation. In-spiration concerns the way in which God gives us Scripture, and how it originally came to be written. Interpretation concerns the way in which man receives it, and how it is to be understood and applied.

It needs to be said at once that we cannot understand all Scripture on the same level, but have to take into account the literary form used, the style and status of the writers themselves, the historical context, and the relation of one part of Scripture to the rest. For instance, it is perfectly clear at times that we are reading what is meant to be taken literally, and at others what is poetical, figurative or symbolical. It is true that there are occasions when we cannot be quite sure which form the writer intends us to infer, but in reading Scripture we have to be alive to this change which, while it does not affect the inspiration of what we read, may appreciably affect our understanding and application.

Then again, we have to distinguish between the recorded words and the sentiments expressed. Obviously what the enemies of God's people said, or the false prophets, or the accusers of Jesus was not inspired in the sense that it expressed the mind of God. What was inspired was the recording of these remarks. As John Stott puts it in his *Understanding the Bible*, when referring to some of the things which Job and his comforters said in the first thirty-seven chapters of that book, 'It is recorded in order to be contradicted, not in order to be believed.'

Once again, there is a grey area where it is sometimes necessary to admit ignorance, because we are unable to be quite certain whether we are listening to man's recording of God's voice or God's recording of man's. What are we to make, for example, of those expressions of despair, disbelief and even vengeance, particularly in the psalms, made by men who in other respects were devoted servants of the Lord? It is my own belief that it does not interfere with the doctrine of inspiration to suppose that God permitted such passages to be set down, not to provide us with an example to follow, nor either to approve or condemn the sentiments expressed, but rather to show us what loneliness, sorrow, pain and anguish can do to the spirit of man apart from the grace of God.

Then again, we must study the historical context. We shall not expect standards which were only fully revealed in Jesus Christ to apply when assessing the conduct of people living in the middle bronze age, and we can only discern the permanent principles involved when we relate the narrative to the conditions prevailing at the time. In our eyes, for example, the way in which Elijah treated the prophets of Baal (1 Kings 18) was unnecessarily savage and severe. But that is an historical judgement. What is of eternal value in the story is his wholehearted determination to purify the country of everything that offended the white-hot holiness of God.

Prophecy too presents us with a problem. Sometimes it

seems that the prophet is looking into the distant future and does not even know the significance of what he is saying (1 Pet. 1. 10–12); but at other times his pronouncements seem to bear a double interpretation, applying at one level to the people of his own time, and at another level to some future generation. We have already observed the same thing in relation to the predictions of Jesus Himself. There are those which refer to the fall of Jerusalem in AD 70, and there are those which look right ahead to His own return. Sometimes, perhaps, He is referring to both at once.

It is very important too that we should as far as possible allow Scripture to interpret itself, by comparing one part of it with another. There will be times when one passage, taken by itself, only gives us one side of the picture, and must be supplemented by others. For example in Exodus 24.10 we are told quite plainly that Moses and those with him 'saw the God of Israel', but in John 1.18 we learn with equal emphasis that 'no man has seen God at any time'. Such apparent contradictions are not difficult to reconcile. God can reveal Himself to man in terms which he can understand without disclosing what human eyes could never look upon, namely His essential being. A man who has only heard an organ transcription of 'The Unfinished Symphony' is being equally truthful when he says that he has and that he has not heard it. Many contradictions disappear with this kind of treatment; and when we relate Scripture to itself in this way, we not only arrive at a balance of truth, but we discover its inner unity.

But it may be asked by some, 'To which of the many versions of Scripture does all that has been said about authority and inspiration apply?' The answer must be that it can only apply to Scripture as originally given. There is nothing sacrosanct about any of the hundreds of versions which have been produced, including the so-called 'Authorized Version', for the word applies, of course, not to its intrinsic value, but to the fact that it was a translation commanded by James I.

Quite apart from erroneous and even tendentious translations, there is the problem created for all translators as to whether they should be governed by what is known as 'literal' or 'dynamic equivalence'. We are aware of this difficulty in modern languages. No doubt most countries have a phrase which is equivalent to our expression – 'to pull your leg', but to translate it literally would probably cause much confusion, and it is necessary to look for an idiom which will convey the precise meaning, but probably in completely different words.

This is even more of a problem when it comes to translating ancient languages, because you have to bring them up-to-date as well as into another culture. On the whole the Authorized and some of the older versions tended to opt for literal equivalence, which is partly why they are harder to understand. Probably most of us can remember being puzzled by the phrase in Matthew 1.25 – 'and he knew her not' *(kai ouk eginosken auteen)* referring to the relationship between Joseph and Mary after he had discovered that she was expecting the child Jesus. Twenty years ago, perhaps, the dynamic equivalent would have been, 'and he had no sexual intercourse with her'; while today we might say, 'and he did not make love to her'.

It is the general practice of the modern translators to choose this rather than the literal way of rendering the original text. It makes the Bible more readable, if sometimes less euphonious, and brings it home with a more powerful impact; but of course we cannot claim inspiration for the result, which is why the study of Hebrew and Greek is of such immense value to the true Bible scholar.

But in all this, we must remember that the Bible is essentially a practical book, appealing as much to the heart of man as to his head. It compares itself to the food (Deut. 8.3; 1 Pet. 2.2) by which our spiritual lives are nourished and develop; the mirror, which reveals and corrects our faults (Jas. 1.23); the sword, with which we may fight the battles of temptation and doubt (Eph. 6.17; Heb. 4.12); the map, by which we find our way (Josh. 1.8); and the lamp for our path (Psa. 119.105).

All these metaphors suggest ways in which the Bible can be of essentially practical value to the Christian, but they all carry with them the need for a responsive action on our part if we are to benefit from them. We must eat the food, use the mirror, sharpen the sword, consult the map and focus the lamp. In other words, we must become regular and consistent readers of this book.

Most people have found it helpful to study the Bible in

two ways: textually and topically. It is wise to take one book of the Bible at a time, and to study it carefully with the aid of a good commentary or explanatory notes; and at the same time to take different themes, such as prayer, temptation, service and so on, and trace the teaching on these subjects throughout the Bible. By taking this double view of the Bible, and studying, as it were, the transverse and the longitudinal sections, we will derive the greatest benefit, and also get a balanced, overall picture of its teaching.

In closing there are two important things to remember. The first is that the full enjoyment of the Bible belongs to those who have made a genuine start in the Christian life. I referred earlier to a map, which only begins to make sense and to have meaning for those exploring the country it represents. We might also compare the Bible to a stained-glass window. Looked at from the outside, people may admire its shape and size, just as they admire the beauty of the language of the Bible; but the full glory of that window will only be experienced by those who enter the building itself. In the same way, the Bible is a book for people who are, so to speak, 'on the inside': who have begun the Christian life, and have come into a personal experience of the Author's love and power.

Finally, we must remember that because it is the Holy Spirit who inspired the writings, it is only He who can fully interpret and apply them. A tour of St Paul's Cathedral, conducted by Sir Christopher Wren himself, would be the most marvellous eye-opener; and that is what the Holy Spirit is waiting and wanting to do for us with regard to the Scriptures. The Bible is like a sundial, an attractive object to have in the garden, but little more than that until the sun comes out, when the ornament is turned into an instrument; and that is what the Holy Spirit can do to the Bible. That is why it is always so important to seek His help when starting to read, and why a sincerely worded prayer will bring the illumination we need.

8   The Church – Its Nature

The word 'Church' has two meanings. The word itself, and its Scottish equivalent 'Kirk', come from the Greek word *Kuriakos* which simply means 'the Lord's', and was later used in a phrase like *Kuriakon doma* ('the Lord's house' – the building where Christians met) ; or *Kuriake hemera* ('the Lord's day').

But in the New Testament the word translated 'Church' is *Ekklesia* (which gives us the French *Eglise* and the Italian *Inglesa*). It comes from a word meaning to 'call out', and is used to describe the local assembly of Christians, but never the actual building where they meet. The word was not peculiar to Christian gatherings, and was also used in other contexts to describe any congregation of people met together for a particular purpose, and perhaps summoned by a herald. For example, we find the word used of 'the assembly' which gathered together in the theatre at Ephesus to demonstrate against Paul (Acts 19.31–32).

In the Greek translation of the Old Testament, known as the *Septuagint* (LXX), the word *ekklesia* is used to describe the whole community of the people of God, whether assembled together or not. They were those whom He had 'called out of Egypt': 'When Israel was a child, then I loved him, and called my son out of Egypt' (Hos. 11.1). It was only natural, therefore, that the word should be taken over in the New Testament and used to describe those whom Christ had called out of the world to be His followers and disciples (Matt. 16.18; 18.17).

It is therefore in this second sense, as a gathering of people and not as a local building, that we shall be studying the meaning of the Church: its nature in this chapter and its functions in the next; but before we do so we must clear up one or two misunderstandings.

First, we must distinguish between the Church and its ordained ministry. 'I have decided to go into the church', I said to my headmaster, when I had made up my mind to be a clergyman, and wanted to give up science for history. Very promptly and rightly he corrected me, pointing out that I was a member of the church already, and that what I was proposing to do was to seek to enter the ministry of the church. I have never made that mistake again, although on scores of occasions I have heard it made, and have grown tired of trying to correct it.

We see this distinction quite clearly in Mark 3.13, 14. 'Jesus goes up into a mountain, and calls to Himself whom He would and they come to Him' — there you have the beginning of the church, the original tiny spring from which the river rose. 'And He ordained twelve, that they should be with Him, and that He might send them forth to preach . . . ' — there you have the beginning of the ministry of the church, its specially ordained or commissioned servants.

The second distinction which we must make is between what is sometimes called the 'visible' and the 'invisible' church. I am not here referring to the living and the dead, though these words are sometimes used to make this distinction; but to the fact that the true church (invisible) is not necessarily to be identified with all those who attend church (visible). The parable of the wheat and the tares (Matt. 13.24–30, 36–40) warns us against making any premature judgement in this matter, between those who possess the faith and those who merely profess; for this is a distinction which can only finally be known to God Himself.

But that there is this distinction is a fact of life. We see it very clearly in the life of the church overseas, in undeveloped countries. The first generation of Church members are all convinced Christians, but by the second and third generations the community has become 'christianized' in a less positive and definite way. Attached to the true church there are hangers-on and fellow travellers, those, that is, who give it their sympathy and, as it were, 'their vote', without ever becoming fully committed members of it.

This leads us directly to the question, What qualifies me for membership of the church? From the very earliest days people of all ages, classes and types started to join the church, but though their starting-points and experiences were different, there seemed to be a sort of common entrance. They all came in by the same gate of repentance and faith (Acts

20.21), of which the outward sign was baptism and the
continuing evidence was a life which was pleasing to God.
Thus the word which quickly came to be used to describe
church members was 'believers' (Acts 5.14; 1 Tim. 4.12), a
word which is enjoying revived popularity today, in an age
of scepticism, especially in some Eastern European countries.

A third distinction which we need to observe is that
between the church triumphant in heaven and the church
militant here on earth. The New Testament does not recognize death as more than a frontier, and Christians who have
died are rather like British citizens who have gone to live
abroad. Spiritually they are still part of the same 'united'
kingdom, and eager witnesses of events that are taking place
on earth (Heb. 12.1, 2). The Church of England, in its
service of Holy Communion (1662) draws particular attention to this fact, and invites all those present to join 'with all
the company of heaven' in praising and worshipping God.
And the same idea is finely expressed in the Bidding Prayer
used on Christmas Eve at the Carol Service in King's College
Chapel at Cambridge, when we are asked to remember 'all
those who rejoice with us, but upon another shore and in a
greater light: that company which no man can number,
whose hope was in the word made flesh, and with whom, in
this Lord Jesus, we are for ever one.'

As we turn now to study the nature of the church, perhaps
the most effective way of doing so, as well as the simplest,
is to take the four metaphors which Paul uses in Ephesians,
and which are developed by himself and others in different
parts of the New Testament: A building, a brotherhood (or
family) a body and a bride.

When Paul speaks of the church as a *building* (Eph. 2.19–
22) in this context, he is of course using the word meta-
phorically, and is not thinking of a material edifice ('*kuriakon
doma*'), but of a spiritual building. Individual Christians are
the bricks or stones, bound together by the mortar of their
love for Christ; and the foundation is the apostles and
prophets, Jesus Christ Himself being the chief corner-stone.

This building, the Christian church, is one of the dwelling-
places of the Holy Spirit – 'an habitation of God through the
Spirit'. Jesus Himself anticipated this when He promised to
be present in a special way when just a handful of people
were gathered together in His name (Matt. 18.20), and

there is a corporate as well as an individual sense in which Christians may enjoy the presence of the Holy Spirit. Once again Cranmer recognized this in a much misunderstood prayer which appears in the Book of Common Prayer: 'And take not Thy Holy Spirit from us'. The Holy Spirit will never leave us as individuals, but He can withdraw His special presence from a community, if He is resisted, quenched or grieved.

Peter develops this idea further (1 Pet. 2), by explaining the two main functions of this spiritual building. They are to 'offer up' (5) and to 'show forth' (9): worship and witness. This has always been the twofold task of the Christian church. It must reach upwards to God and outwards to the world; and we shall return to this subject in the next chapter.

In Paul's next chapter to the Ephesians, we have a picture of the church as a *brotherhood* (Eph. 3), or family. One of the earliest words used to describe Christians was 'brethren'. In fact is was frequently used by Jesus Himself, and He defined brethren as those who 'hear the word of God and do it' (Luke 8.21). He thought of God as the Father of the family, and of Himself as the eldest brother; and in fact Paul in one place describes Him as 'the first-born among many brethren' (Rom. 8.29) to whose likeness the rest of the family should conform.

The thought suggested by this particular metaphor is that of fellowship, the Greek word for which (*koinonia*) contains the basic idea of sharing, and outside the New Testament is used of the marriage relationship and of business partnerships.

The early Christians experimented with a literal sharing of possessions, and lived for a time as a kind of commune or kibbutz (Acts 4.31–37). It is perhaps doubtful whether such an arrangement can be sustained on a large scale or for an indefinite period, but there are many examples throughout history, and at the present time, of small — and possibly temporary — groups living in this way.

But 'sharing' is and always should be a hall-mark of true family life: the house, the garden, the food, the facilities being equally enjoyed by all its members; and the Christian church is called upon to do the same. This does not only mean generosity with our material possessions, though the Bible emphasizes the need for this (Gal. 6.10), but with our

time, our experience, our 'know-how'. There is a danger in
these days of churches allowing fellowship to exist only on
separate levels: the Old People's Club, the Youth Fellowship,
and so on. Obviously there is a place for such things, but the
ideal family is vertical and not horizontal in its structure.
The Church Council, for example, should be composed of
members whose ages stretch from 70-plus to 20-minus. 'Your
old men', says the prophet Joel, 'shall dream dreams, and
your young men shall see visions' (Joel 2.28). Every church
needs both – experience and enthusiasm. It is greatly enriched if it can find scope for both young and old, and if,
learning from each other, they can work together in fellowship.

Paul's next metaphor is perhaps his best known, because
he makes great use of it elsewhere. It is the *body* (Eph. 4).
The Christian church is the corporate entity through which
Christ works in the world today: the body of which He is the
Head.

The thought conveyed by this particular metaphor is
paradoxical: variety and unity. There are no two parts of
the human body which fulfil the same function, and yet the
malfunctioning of any one part, however insignificant, can
weaken the health and spoil the happiness of the whole body,
disinclining it for active service (1 Cor. 12).

The unity of the church is something that has to be
striven for if it is to be maintained. The variety of gifts which
God bestowed upon Christians, giving some more and some
less important parts to play, means that pride and envy
have to be resisted, lest they impair and even destroy that
unity.

Paul is very aware of this danger, and in this same chapter
(Eph. 4) he reminds his readers of the two great unifying
factors in the Christian church: 'The unity of the Spirit' (3)
and 'the unity of the Faith' (13). In other words, unity is
enjoyed by Christians in whose midst the Holy Spirit is
allowed unhindered sovereignty and who also hold in common the great basic truths of their Faith. We hear a great
deal in these days about ecumenicity, and it is clearly the
duty of all the churches to strive towards a great understanding and unity. But it would be foolish to suppose that there is
any short-cut to that end, or that we can by-pass the two
fundamental conditions mentioned above.

A church where variety and unity are held in perfect equilibrium is bound to be a healthy church, and a healthy church is one where we can be sure to find two things: sympathy and activity. There is sympathy, because 'if one member suffers, then all the members suffer with it' (1 Cor. 12.26); and a burden shared is a burden halved, quartered, tithed, according to the number of other Christians who can lighten it through prayerful understanding. And there is activity, because a Christian community where there is no prayer meeting, no opportunity for united Bible study, no evangelistic thrust into the surrounding neighbourhood is not a body, but a corpse.

The last of Paul's four metaphors is that of the *bride* (Eph. 5), and it is one which is adopted by John in the Book of Revelation, where the church is pictured as a bride prepared for her wedding, the Bridegroom, of course, being Christ Himself (Rev. 21.2; 22.17); for 'from heaven He came and sought her to be His holy bride; with His own blood He bought her, and for her sake He died.'

This metaphor is not peculiar to the New Testament, but one which the writers have borrowed from the Old Testament and enriched. It was a great favourite of some of the prophets, notably, perhaps, Hosea: 'I will betroth thee unto me in faithfulness, and thou shalt know the Lord' (Hos. 2.19, 20). Indeed, Hosea's whole prophecy is based upon this metaphor. Israel (the Old Testament equivalent of the Christian church) had deserted her husband (the Lord) and gone after other men (idols), but although He could not overlook, far less condone, such behaviour, yet if she will repent and return to the Lord, He will have mercy, and take her to Himself again; and the prophecy ends with a beautiful picture of those twin characteristics of the perfect marriage: faithfulness and fruitfulness (Hos. 14).

First and fundamentally, the church is called to be faithful, to keep herself only for the Lord. But alas! Her history is a tragic one of continual lapses from the high standard of loyalty expected of her, and again and again she has been drawn away and seduced by heresy.

By and large heresy takes two forms, and has done so from the earliest New Testament days. There are those who feel that they must add to the teaching of Christ, and there are those who feel that they must subtract from it. Paul had

to deal with the first kind of heresy, and the Apostle John
with the second.

Paul had to face the Judaizers who wanted the Gospel-
plus. His epistle to the Galatians is an all-out attack upon
their position, as he tried to show them that things like
circumcision, and various taboos and prohibitions had no
part to play in the salvation of souls. John on the other
hand had to deal with the Gnostics who wanted the Gospel-
minus. They denied that Jesus had assumed a properly
human body and had died, claiming that He had either just
temporarily inhabited a human being, or assumed a merely
phantasmal human appearance. This is why in John's first
epistle there is such powerful emphasis upon the incarnation.

The same seductive temptations face the Christian church
today. The ritualist feels that he must add to the simplicity
that is in Christ. 'Yes', we are told, 'the simple gospel is all
very well, but there are richer insights which tradition has
to offer. We don't want to detract from what you have to
preach, we want to add to it.' But in doing so they blur the
clarity with which people can see the truth of the gospel,
and they muffle its distinctive sound.

The radical pulls the other way. His complaint is not that
the gospel is too simple, but that it is too complicated. He
wants to make it easier for people to become Christians by
stripping the faith of many of its supernatural elements.
'Why complicate matters,' he asks, 'by expecting people to
believe in a virgin birth, a physical resurrection and a literal
ascension? Let us get back to the simple, historical Jesus.'

It is not easy for the young Christian to stand his ground
in these circumstances, to remain faithful to his Lord, and
not to 'hearken to the voice of the charmers, however
cunning their charms may be' (Psa. 58.5). What makes it
even more difficult is that the charmers sometimes operate
from within the recognizable church. It would be easier if
they beckoned to us from beyond its borders, but as it is they
imply that we can be faithful to the Lord while at the same
time still attending to their blandishments.

But of course the church does have to fight on two fronts,
because it is also enticed from without. 'The world is ever
near; we see the sights that dazzle, the tempting sounds we
hear.' Throughout history the church has reacted to the
world in two opposite ways. Sometimes it has become too

isolated from society, and sometimes too involved with it and infected by it.

In the middle ages it was to the first of these temptations that it tended to succumb. In many cases it became too isolated from the life of the ordinary people, retreating into the ivory tower of monasticism. We can appreciate the reason. It was anxious to preserve its purity, and keep itself unspotted from the world (Jas. 1.27).

But is it the opposite danger which faces the Christian church today — to become too involved and identified with the world? Again, we can appreciate the reason; for if the church is to influence society it cannot do so from a distance. The salt is no good if it is kept in the salt-cellar. Jesus did not want to take His followers out of the world (John 17.15); and Paul on one occasion was careful to draw a distinction between separation and isolation (1 Cor. 5.9, 10).

But is it in danger today of losing its distinctively spiritual edge, and of becoming like the salt that has lost its savour, and is trampled under foot as useless? This seemed to be the fear of Edward Norman in his 1978 Reith Lectures. 'The church is increasingly preoccupied with the pursuit of a more just society, and with the material problems of humanity. Secular programmes for human improvement seem more important, as practical if unconscious expressions of God's love, than does the cultivation of correct religious belief.' What he calls the 'politicization of Christianity', by which he means the providing of purely secular policies with a Christian gloss, is in his view one of the most seductive modern heresies.

It is difficult for the Christian church to keep its balance in the midst of all these pressures and problems. It has to steer a middle course between the Scylla of pietism and the Charybdis of secularization. It must be in the world, but not of it. It must be involved without being identified with the world, and at the same time insulated without being isolated. Perhaps the best motto it can take for itself is, 'Go where danger is, but go armed.'

Faithfulness is one mark of the bride, and the other is fruitfulness. The ancient command, the first of all God's commands, was simply this: 'Be fruitful and multiply' (Gen. 1.28). It was God's first word to His creation, and it is one of His first words to His church: 'I have ordained you, that you should go and bring forth fruit, and that your fruit should remain' (John 15.16).

But what is the fruit which God expects to see as a result of this marriage between Christ and His church? In Paul's view it was simply the people whom he was able, with God's help, to bring into the world of Christian faith and experience. In one place he pictures himself as the expectant mother, travailing in birth for her children (Gal. 4.19); while he regarded Timothy (2 Tim 2.1) and Onesimus (Philem. 10) as his spiritual sons; and it was this kind of fruit that he looked forward to producing in Rome, once he had been able to set foot in that city. (Rom. 1.13).

*   *   *

In the light of what has been said so far, it is particularly fascinating to study the letters of the Seven Churches in the early chapters of the Book of Revelation. Here we have seven recently established Christian communities fighting for their survival and their very existence in the midst of a hostile pagan world. In each case John finds something to commend and something to condemn, but taking them altogether, we find that there are three principal threats to their progress: persecution, distraction and corruption.

And so it has always been. At certain periods of history and in certain countries today persecution is what the Christian church has to face. To be a committed member of a Christian group is to invite ostracism, expulsion, and even violence to oneself and one's family. Such people indeed live 'where Satan's seat is' (Rev. 2.13), and they need all the grace and courage that God can give them, and the prayers of His people, if they are to be 'faithful unto death' (Rev. 2.10).

Others face the distraction in the shape of heresy which we have been thinking about: 'by schisms rent asunder, by heresies distressed.' In the days when John was writing it was a sect called 'the Nicolaitines' who were trying to seduce the Christians with doctrinal errors and distractions. For us today it may be those who want to preach what Paul calls 'another gospel: which is not another' (Gal. 1.6, 7). To such Christians the challenge comes, 'Hold fast that which you have' (Rev. 3.11).

And then again, there is the danger of corruption. It is all too easy to allow the influence of things like comfort, materialism, money and social ambition to seep into the life of the Christian church, and into individual lives as well. We lose that first love (Rev. 2.4). We grow lukewarm (Rev. 3.16). The marriage is not broken. It is not seriously threatened. But it begins to go stale, lack-lustre and dull. 'Be zealous, therefore', says John, 'and repent' (Rev. 3.19).

9 The Church – Its Function

In the last chapter we saw that the twofold function of the Christian church is Worship and Witness: to 'offer up spiritual sacrifices acceptable to God' and to 'shew forth the excellencies of Him who has called us out of darkness into His marvellous light' (1 Pet. 2.5, 9). In performing these two functions, Christians take over the Old Testament duties of both priest and prophet; the priest standing on the Godward side of man, and the prophet on the manward side of God. We must now look at these in a little more detail.

The Church of England has been criticized for apparently arrogating to itself the word 'priest', with its sacerdotal overtones, and applying it to one of its three ministerial orders – Bishops, *Priests* and Deacons – when in the New Testament it is never used of Christian ministers, but always of the Christian community as a whole (1 Peter 2.5, 9; Rev. 5.10). Unfortunately the word 'priest' has two meanings. In the New Testament it is used to translate the Greek word *iereus,* with his sacrificial duties; while in Old English it became the accepted contraction of 'presbyter' (Greek: *presbuteros*) or 'elder'; and it is in this sense that it should be understood in the use made of it in the Church of England, where the three orders are Bishops, *Elders,* and Deacons.

The Dictionary reminds us that the original meaning of the word 'worship' was related to the recognition given to men and women of worth or merit; and it still lingers on in this sense when we use it to address a local dignitary, a mayor or magistrate, as 'His Worship'.

But the essential idea behind the word 'worship', in both Old and New Testaments, is that of service. In both Hebrew and Greek the words used for worship signify the service rendered by slaves or hired servants which is accompanied by reverence, homage and fear. Sometimes the words seem to be interchangeable (Cf. Heb. 12.28 AV with RSV), and you still see on some church notice boards the phrase 'Divine Service' where others might use the single word 'Worship'; while in the Church of England Marriage Service of 1662 there appear the words, 'with my body I thee worship', meaning 'serve with honour'.

In its simplest and basic form, therefore, worship is any expression which the believer makes, either by word or deed, which indicates an attitude of reverence and homage to God. A gift, a prayer, a hymn, an act of social kindness, if it is done in this spirit, is automatically an act of worship.

We can worship God, for example, *with our hands*, by the gifts and sacrifices we make to Him. We read of the wise men that when 'they saw the child . . . they fell down and worshipped Him. Then, opening their treasures, they offered Him gifts . . .' (Matt. 2.11). And when Abraham was about to offer up his son, Isaac, as a sacrifice, he turned to his servant and said, 'Stay here with the ass; I and the lad will go yonder and worship, and come again to you' (Gen. 22.5). Time, money, energy gladly and freely given to God for use in His service are a very practical way of showing that we honour Him, and are therefore an important element in worship.

Again, we can worship God *by our lives*. In one version of the Bible we are told to 'worship the Lord in the beauty of holiness' (Psa. 29.2). There are those who get this the wrong way round, and think that it really says, 'worship the Lord in the holiness of beauty'. It is true, of course, that great music, painting and flowers, as well as things like drama and dancing, can enrich and enliven what we do for God; but what He most wants to see, and what gives Him the greatest pleasure, is holiness of life. It is when He sees in us a likeness to His Son, and a mini-reflection of Himself that He feels most honoured.

And we can worship God *through our lips*; for praise (Psa. 66.4), prayer and song are very important ways of showing God what we think He is worth. This is what the prophet Hosea calls in one place 'the fruit of our lips' (Hos. 14.2), and it is interesting to notice how often in the Bible we are encouraged to shout and sing as a way of giving God the honour and glory which are His due.

Although it has this breadth of meaning, it is this last aspect of the word, namely what we do together in church,

that has become associated in the minds of most people with
the idea of worship. In the very early days it was largely an
individual act, as we see from the experience of Abraham's
servant when he met Rebekah (Gen. 24.26) and from
Jacob at Bethel (Gen. 28. 10–22) ; but as we move on from
the simple patriarchal days, we find that certain forms of
worship become more congregational, with people getting
together, with greater ritual and formality, to express their
praise and gratitude to God, to make their requests known
to Him and to hear His word (1 Chron. 29.20). The temple
in Jerusalem became the focal point for this worship, or
divine service, until its destruction led to the development of
the simpler form of worship in the synagogues, which continued even after the building of Herod's temple.

But it is interesting to note that for the Christians nothing
at first took the place either of synagogue or temple. The
first day of the week was observed as the Lord's Day, in
honour of His resurrection, and took the place of the Jewish
Sabbath, but nothing more formal seems to have developed
than local house groups (Philem. 2) where Christians met
together for singing, prayer, and the exercise of spiritual
gifts (Eph. 5.19; Col. 3.16; 1 Cor. 14.26–33). The *Agape* or
'Love Feast' became a regular feature of these gatherings,
and was usually followed by the Lord's Supper (1 Cor.
11.23–28), but the New Testament closes without anything
established in the way of formal patterns of worship to
which we can trace the sort of services enjoyed in many
churches today.

It is partly because of this lack of any firm Scriptural
pattern that there is such a wide variety of forms of worship
in our different churches today, varying from the very
formal to the almost casual; and it is difficult, and perhaps
unnecessary to try to argue from Scripture that one is right
and another wrong. Indeed, the very variety itself is to be
welcomed in that it appeals to a wide range of tastes and
temperaments. The pity is when fairly superficial differences
are allowed to crystallize into doctrines and principles, and
when Christians feel they must take up and defend en-
trenched positions. It was Hugh Redwood who said that
he thought divisions within the church were to be welcomed, provided we learned to use them not as political
divisions, but as military, engaging the enemy on as

many different fronts as possible.

There are of course certain features which are common to services in every church. There are opportunities for prayer, for hymn singing, for Bible reading and for preaching; and however formal or informal the style may be, all Christians would agree that a time of united worship was defective if it did not include all these ingredients.

Finally, and before we leave this subject, it needs to be said that worship must be *from our hearts*. The Lord complained to Isaiah of those people who 'draw near with their mouth and honour me with their lips, while their hearts are far from me' (Isa. 29.13); and Ezekiel expressed God's disapproval of those who 'with their lips show much love, but their heart is set on gain' (Ezek. 33.31). The outward form was not matched by the inner spirit. They were adopting towards God the attitude of the play-actor or hypocrite, a respectable veneer masking their real feelings. Such service is unacceptable to God who insists that those who worship Him must do so 'in spirit and in truth' (John 4.24).

*   *   *

We must now turn to the second primary function of the Christian church — showing forth rather than offering up. Just as the Holy Spirit is Christ's ambassador to the believers, so the church is His ambassador to the unbelievers (2 Cor. 5.20); for humanly speaking it is the only means of communication He has with the world, and the only way in which He can be represented there, and His message heard.

There is a legend that upon His return to heaven at the Ascension, Jesus was met by one of the angels and questioned concerning the plans He had made for the continuation of His work on earth. He explained that He had left behind Him eleven men to whom He had entrusted His message. The angel drew attention to their human frailty, and asked what would happen if they were to fail. 'If they fail,' replied the Lord Jesus, 'I have no other plans.'

Fortunately for us they did not fail, and the gospel reached our own shores; but the same principle operates today. The church is God's only way of reaching the world, and if we fail, then He has no other plans. It is true that occasionally one hears of someone who becomes a Christian apparently

without any human assistance. Saul of Tarsus was perhaps
a case in point, though it is doubtful whether he would ever
have become spiritually air-borne if it had not been for the
help which he received first from Ananias, and later on from
Barnabas.

It is interesting to note the contrast between the first
recorded words of Jesus to His disciples and the last. Meeting them at the outset of His ministry, He said, 'Come . . . '
(John 1.39); while taking leave of them for the last time He
turned to them and said, 'Go . . . ' (Matt. 28.20). Having
obeyed the first command, it is the church's duty to obey the
second. Having come in for strength, it must go out for
service; having come in to discover, it must now go out to
declare.

It follows that a church which is not continually trying
to reach across its frontiers to the regions beyond is failing
in one of its most important responsibilities; and the same
applies to a Christian who has never lifted up his eyes and
looked upon the fields, and seen that they are 'white already
to harvest' (John 4.35).

But what, we may ask, was the motive which compelled
eleven very ordinary men to abandon their former way of
life, and devote the rest of their days to spreading the news
about Jesus Christ, often at the risk of liberty and life itself?
Paul, who later took such a leading part in evangelism,
supplies the answer. 'The love of Christ constrains us', he
said (2 Cor. 5.14). The word he uses *(sunecho)* is that
which Luke uses on two occasions, when he says that Simon
Peter's mother-in-law is 'taken' with a great fever (Luke
4.38) and when he speaks of the multitude 'thronging' Jesus
(Luke 8.45). So, says Paul, the love of Christ, demonstrated
upon the cross in such a wonderful way, sweeps us off our
feet and completely masters us.

It is doubtful whether any other motive would have been
strong enough. Men will do and dare great things in the
cause of duty, or for the sake of ambition or even money;
but it has always been love that has called forth the most
sustained and noblest acts of heroism and devotion. That
is certainly how it was with the early Christians and how it
should be with us. It drove them out of their homes and
countries, seeking everywhere for those who without Christ
they knew to be eternally forlorn, and doing so in the teeth

of every imaginable hazard.

So much for the ambassador's motive, but now what about his message? For he is the channel through whom one kingdom speaks to another, in this case the kingdom of light to the kingdom of darkness. A long-forgotten report appeared at the end of the war called 'Towards the Conversion of England'. It had been commissioned by the two Archbishops of the day, and it defined evangelism as follows: 'To evangelize is so to present Christ Jesus in the power of the Holy Spirit, that men shall come to put their trust in God through Him, to accept Him as their Saviour, and serve Him as their King in the fellowship of His Church.' Nearly forty years later it would be difficult to improve on that definition; for the eternal gospel does not change, and it is still our responsibility to offer Christ to people as Saviour and King, and to invite them to enjoy a life of Service and Fellowship.

Having considered the motive and the message, let us look briefly at the men – the individual ambassadors. We must remember that we are representatives as well as messengers. Our king and country are judged by our character as well as by our communications, and we shall earn no respect for our message which we do not earn as men of God.

If people feel that they can look towards Christians, either as a body or as individuals, for the kindness, the sympathy and understanding they feel they need, then they are going to be far more strongly attracted to the gospel which we have to preach. Love is the *lingua franca* of all Christian service, a language which does not need to be translated, because it is understood by people of every nation and of all ages.

We must now turn to methods, and consider the ways in which the gospel can be conveyed to others. While it is perfectly true to say that the gospel cannot alter, the method of its presentation does and should; for what is appropriate for one generation or for one country may be unsuitable at a different time and in another place. There is no reason why today, for example, all the modern means of communication should not be mobilized in the service of the gospel; and if films, drama, ballet and puppetry – to name but some – help to convey the gospel to those who might otherwise never even want to hear it, then they should certainly be used.

But of course techniques of this sort are transient. They were undreamed of fifty years ago in this context, and in fifty years' time they may well be superseded by others; and it would appear that the two most permanent forms of communication are writing and preaching, both of which have been used from New Testament days onwards.

We are told that letter-writing is a lost art, killed by the telephone and the motor car which make it much easier than it used to be to talk to and to meet our friends. It is sad if this is so, because the thought that can be put into a letter and the time that can be taken to peruse it make it a uniquely valuable form of personal communication. It was in this way that Paul and the other apostles prepared the way for the gospel, and laid the foundations for the great spiritual advance of the first century; and many later generations of evangelists have used it to great effect.

But if letter-writing is less popular than it used to be, the scale on which Christian literature is now produced is phenomenal, and the well chosen book, given to the right person at the right time, can be of enormous value; and there are many who would testify to the fact that it was through reading some book by a Christian author that spiritually speaking they first saw the light of day.

But by and large it is still through preaching that the gospel is most effectively transmitted. There are six Greek words which are used in the New Testament and which are translated by the English word 'preaching'. One conveys the idea of arguing and disputing, and is used to describe Paul's seminars at Ephesus and elsewhere (Acts 18.19). Another is the word which in classical Greek simply means to 'chat'. In the New Testament it has a more dignified meaning, but is probably intended to convey the idea of a less formal kind of talk, as we may infer from a study of the words used in Acts 8.25. But the other four words all mean 'proclamation', 'declaration' and 'announcement', and are by far the most common. This is not surprising, for we may question whether there can be any very effective 'disputation' or 'chatter' if there has not been an initial 'pronouncement'.

This then lies at the root of all evangelistic preaching. It is the proclamation of good news. In the early days of the BBC we used to speak of a News Announcer, but nowadays

for some reason he has become a News Reader or even a
News Caster. But the phrase 'News Announcer' exactly
describes the Christian preacher. Like the Herald or Town
Crier of old, he has news, and good news at that, to impart
to all who will listen. The argument, the reasoning, the
chatter will follow as a matter of course, when the crowd
breaks up into twos and threes; but first people must be clear
what they are arguing and chatting about, and they can only
learn this from the preacher.

'Preach to reach each' is a motto some ministers take as
their own, and it is a good one. It does not mean that we can
appeal to all the people all the time. The purpose of preaching is not 'by some means to save all', but 'by all means to
save some' (1 Cor. 9.22); and this will mean that we are to
understand those who are listening to us, their age, culture,
outlook and background.

But more importantly, it will mean an understanding of
what constitutes a person as an individual. It seems clear
from many parts of the Bible that everyone presents the
preacher with four distinct targets — the mind, the conscience, the heart and the will; and the good sermon, or
series of sermons, will make sure that none of these is lost
sight of.

First, our preaching must be reasoned. The person or
people we are addressing must be able to say, 'I see'. It is
worth noting that when Jesus appeared to His disciples in
the upper room after His resurrection, it was their 'understanding' which He enlightened; and Philip's first remark
to the Ethiopian whom he was led to counsel was not, as we
might have expected, 'Do you believe what you have read?'
but 'Do you understand it?' (Acts 8.30).

Clarity and simplicity are therefore fundamental qualities
for a good preacher, and he will use every device to enable
even the simplest members of his congregation to understand
what he is saying. Speaking to children, he will see the value
of using visual aids; while there are very few adults who do
not prefer to listen to a talk which is verbally well illustrated.

Secondly, our preaching must be moral. People must be
brought to the point of saying, 'I ought'. It is interesting
that Paul, writing to the Corinthians, tells us that he com-
mends himself to 'every man's conscience' (2 Cor. 4.2). The
conscience is the agent inside someone's personality which is

on the side of truth, and will unlock the gate to the invading power of the gospel. It is part of the underground resistance movement and is waiting for the right moment to respond to the challenge from without.

It was David's conscience which lifted the drawbridge for the prophet Nathan, after his squalid affair with Bathsheba (2 Sam. 12). It was Paul's conscience which sabotaged his resistance to the gospel (Acts 9.5). And it was conscience which betrayed those who listened to Peter's great sermon, and forced them to surrender (Acts 2.37).

In the third place there must be an emotional element in our preaching, because we are appealing to the heart which is the very centre of a person's feelings and sensitivity. We need to get to the point at which our hearers will say, 'I want'. It was John Wesley who, on that famous day in May 1738, wrote that he felt his heart 'strangely warmed' and that he did love Christ.

Of course we shall avoid emotionalism – the unhealthy and unnecessary stirring of a sensitive nature which can only in the long run produce an unfavourable reaction. But the gospel carries its own powerful emotional appeal, and we can safely leave it to do its own work without any histrionic embroidery on our part.

Finally, preaching must be practical. We must aim at the will. We want a verdict, and the verdict we want is contained in the two words, 'I do'. This was the immediate response of the Philippian Gaoler on the night of the earthquake. 'What must I do to be saved?' he asked (Acts 16.30). The sort of sermon which leaves the hearers undecided, and not knowing what is expected of them or what to do next, is like the trumpet of which Paul complained (1 Cor. 14.8). Its sound was so vague and uncertain that people did not know what to do. Should they prepare for battle or make for the cook-house door? Or was it the last post?

It is a pity that the word 'preaching' is confined in most people's minds to what is done in the pulpit or on the platform, for often the most telling sermon is preached when the congregation consists of one person, and all that has been said so far applies with equal force whether we are talking to a friend in our homes or to a congregation of hundreds in a cathedral. In every case the sermon must be vertical and not just horizontal. It must move through mind, heart, conscience and will, and evoke the response, I see, I ought, I want and I do.

But going back to our original definition of evangelism, there is one important point we must not overlook. Preaching must be 'in the power of the Holy Spirit'. Paul speaks of 'the foolishness of preaching' (1 Cor. 1.21). It is a curious phrase, and the word he uses is a strong one from which we derive our word 'moron'. There are not many politicians, for example, who would like their speeches described as 'moronic'. What is Paul driving at?

The politician, and most other speakers, like their speeches to have style and panache, and to be laced with wit, humour and anecdote. It does not follow that a sermon which possesses these qualities is any the worse for it, but if that is all it possesses, then it is hollow and worthless; for what makes a sermon powerful and penetrating is not the eloquence of the preacher, but the extent to which it can be used as a weapon in the hands of the Holy Spirit.

This is because it is only the Holy Spirit who can open the minds of people, awaken their consciences, warm their hearts and stir their wills; and the foolishness of preaching to which Paul refers consists in the fact that the Christian preacher does not rely upon those things which the world regards as essential in a speaker, but upon something which the world cannot even begin to understand, namely the presence and power of the Holy Spirit.

A painting by Rubens in the National Gallery depicts the scene described in Numbers 21 and referred to by Jesus in John 3.14, 15. The camp was plagued by poisonous snakes and Moses was told to make a serpent of brass and set it up upon a pole. All who had been bitten were invited to look at the brazen serpent, and as many as did so were cured. In the picture Moses is shown pointing to the brass serpent with one hand, and with the other beckoning to the people to look. Nothing could sum up more aptly the evangelistic task of the Christian church: to point to the cross and to beckon to the world.

10 The Sacraments

The word 'Sacrament' does not appear in the New Testament at all. It comes from a Latin word *Sacramentum* which had two meanings: a pledge, or a deposit, which could be forfeited to charitable purposes, and a soldier's oath. It was sometimes used to translate the Greek word *musterion* (which meant 'a secret to be revealed'), but it was only later on that it began to be applied to Christian rites, and much later when it assumed its present popular meaning of a physical action which signified a mental or spiritual attitude or to use St Augustine's phrase, 'a visible word'.

Understood in this way, the sacramental principle lies at the very roots of our social life; for there are many occasions when we use physical or material means to express our thoughts. There are times, for example, when 'words fail us', and a smile, a wink or a shrug of the shoulders conveys far more accurately than any words could do just what is going on in our minds; and in such cases the smile, or wink, or shrug becomes a sacrament.

And have we not all known times when we are 'too full for words'? We have not been able to trust ourselves to express the joy or anguish we feel, and have been obliged to convey the emotion we experience by touch or gesture? Quite literally, the occasion has been 'too sad' or 'too joyful for words'.

It is because of this that a whole range of 'social sacraments' have developed: the kiss is the outward and visible sign of love, the handshake of friendship, the salute of loyalty and respect, and so on; and it was not long before the Christian church came to see in two particular ceremonies ordained by Christ this same sacramental principle. These are Baptism and the Lord's Supper. The first is the 'sacrament of beginning' and the second the 'sacrament of belonging'.

The Roman Catholic Church has added five other sacraments which it regards as obligatory, but the Reformed

Churches have always maintained that Baptism and the Lord's Supper are the only two actually ordained by Christ, and have an added authority in that they have their roots in the Old Testament, Baptism being the counterpart of the Jewish rite of Circumcision, and Holy Communion of the Passover.

Article XXV of the Church of England describes the sacraments as 'effectual signs of grace', and goes on to say that God uses them to 'work invisibly in us' 'not only to quicken, but also strengthen and confirm our faith in Him.' In other words, faith, which is the only faculty by which the believers can communicate with Christ, is aroused into more conscious activity through the sacraments. They are what have been called 'dynamic symbols', because they stimulate what they express, just as a handshake confirms friendship, or a kiss deepens love and a salute fortifies loyalty.

It is here that perhaps the modern and the ancient meaning of the word 'sacramentum' converge, for very often a sign can be a pledge. A handshake, for example, may seal a pact or agreement, and one of the very earliest sacraments in the Old Testament was the rainbow which God gave as a sign and a pledge that He would not again flood the whole earth. In fact the two words 'sign' and 'pledge' became almost identified in the word 'signature', which is a signed pledge or promise to pay a debt, perhaps, or to transfer property; and the Christian sacraments are occasions when, as it were, God Himself and the Christian believer sign a treaty or covenant. At Baptism we pledge repentance and faith, and God promises regeneration; and at Holy Communion, we pledge 'ourselves, our souls and bodies' to Him in service, and He promises His indwelling presence to sustain us as 'we feed on Him in our hearts by faith'. Ink, of course, is not used for this signature, but water in one case, and bread and wine in the other.

Turning now to *Baptism,* we find that as well as its association with circumcision, already referred to, it is mentioned by both Paul (1 Cor. 10.1, 2) and Peter (1 Pet. 3.18–22) as the means whereby God effected the escape of His people from judgement; and as a rite to mark moral and spiritual reformation, it was practised well before the coming of Christ by certain Jewish Sects, though the first we read of it in the New Testament in this sense is when John the

Baptist called people to turn to God, 'preaching a baptism of repentance for the forgiveness of sins' (Mark 1.4). The candidate for baptism would be immersed in the water and then re-emerge. The immersion was a sign of repentance and the washing away of sin, and the emergence was a sign of the new life to be lived.

With the coming of Christ, the same thoughts continued of repentance, remission and renewal, but baptism now began to acquire a new significance, and to be associated with His death and resurrection. The immersion became a sharing in all the benefits of His death and burial, and the emergence a sharing in His life of resurrection power (Rom. 6.4; Col. 2.12).

With the coming of the Holy Spirit we find that baptism assumes a third dimension; for in Acts 2.38 His indwelling presence is clearly promised to all those (and they numbered three thousand) who in repentance and faith underwent the rite of baptism by water.

It is important to note that from the very earliest days baptism has been administered with the trinitarian formula, 'in the name of the Father, and of the Son, and of the Holy Spirit' (Matt. 28.19); and the significance of this must lie at least partly in the fact that baptism, sincerely received, involves repentance towards God, identification by faith in the death and resurrection of the Lord Jesus, and reception of the Holy Spirit.

Historically, churches have differed from each other as to the age at which baptism should be administered, though in all cases the principles outlined above have lain behind the practice itself. Some of the reformed churches, notably the Church of England and the Presbyterian Churches practise what is called 'paedobaptism', that is, the baptizing of children before they reach the age of understanding. Those who seek to justify this custom do so partly on the grounds of the association between baptism in the New Testament and circumcision in the Old; partly because in the covenant language of the Old Testament there is a tendency to use the present or even the past tense to indicate a future experience (Gen. 15.18); and partly because parents are taught that they have a solemn duty so to teach the child that in due course it will make a conscious commitment to Christ, for which an opportunity is provided in a future service of Confirmation or Dedication.

With regard to the argument as to whether baptism should be by immersion or sprinkling, there is no doubt that in New Testament days it was the former custom that was practised. Sprinkling was probably introduced for practical reasons, in the case of infants or in desert countries, for example, or the very sick; and it is interesting to note that the earliest sub-apostolic account of baptism expressly provides for 'pouring water on the head' where immersion is not to be had.

Before we leave this subject of baptism, it is important to remember what a very effective form of witness it can be. In this country, where so often it has become just a matter of form, we have rather lost sight of this aspect; but in other countries, where it signifies a complete break with some other religion like Hinduism or Islam, to take a public stance for Jesus Christ in this way, can be a most courageous thing to do and represents a complete burning of one's boats.

We must now consider *The Lord's Supper*. It became a very early custom for Christians to meet together for a meal (Acts 2.46; Jude 12), just as others were in the habit of doing who were bound together by social or racial ties. Such gatherings of Christians were known as *Agapai* or 'Love feasts', and the purpose was one of mutual fellowship and encouragement, still seen, perhaps in things like 'Parish Breakfasts' today.

At some stage in the proceedings the leader would probably call for silence, and there would be a solemn moment when bread and wine would be passed round, and eaten and drunk 'in remembrance' of what Christ had done for them upon the cross (Luke 22.19; 1 Cor. 11.23–25). We might compare it to the 'Loyal Toast', as it is called, when the chairman or president at some dinner or banquet asks everyone to stand as he proposes the health of the Sovereign. The separation of the Agape from the Eucharist (or 'Thanksgiving') lies outside the time of the New Testament; and we are not sure just when it was that Christians decided that for them the Lord's Supper should replace the old Jewish Passover, at which they had remembered with gratitude to God their deliverance from the bondage of Egypt (1 Cor. 5.7).

Besides the important part played by grateful remembrance and fellowship, in the sharing of the bread and wine, the sacramental idea in the Lord's Supper went somewhat deeper; for it included the identification of the Christians by faith with their crucified and risen Lord (1 Cor. 11.27–29). As they ate the bread and drank the wine, so they would 'feed on Him in their hearts by faith with thanksgiving'. I always remember a prayer which Dr Chavasse, at one time Bishop of Rochester, was fond of using after a service of Holy Communion in his chapel. 'Grant O Lord, that we who have duly received these holy mysteries may perceive within ourselves the fruits of Thy redemption.' It is in that sort of experience that we see the true sacramental principle at work.

Just as baptism is an act of witness, so also is attendance at Holy Communion, for it is a way of proclaiming the death of Christ to the world outside. As Paul said, 'as often as you eat this bread, and drink this cup, you declare the Lord's death till He come' (1 Cor. 11.26). In other words, by partaking of the Lord's Supper we are actually preaching to others. We are proclaiming the importance we attach to the cross, so that any unbelievers who may be present, or who may simply know that we attend, will see for themselves the central place we give in our thinking to the death of Christ.

The poppy bought on Remembrance Sunday can of course be just a matter of form, and we wear it because it is the done thing, and we would not like to be thought churlish or ungracious by not doing so; but it can have a deep significance if it honestly declares our respect and gratitude for the sacrifice that was made on our behalf by others in the war, perhaps by people we actually knew and loved.

As we saw earlier, one of the original ideas of the word *sacramentum* was a pledge, and the words 'till He come' remind us that the bread and the wine are the outward signs of His promise to do so, when His presence with us will make the continued use of symbols unnecessary.

In a previous chapter we thought of the Christian church as the Bride of Christ, and we might compare the sacrament of Holy Communion to an engagement ring worn by a girl who is shortly to be married to the man she loves. That ring does four things for her. First, it reminds her of a day in the past when love was born. Then it links her in fellowship with others who are enjoying the same experience. Next it declares to the world at large that she is pledged to the man she loves; and finally, it looks forward to the day when his promise is fulfilled, and they will finally be united to each other.

There is a continuing debate on the subject of Christian behaviour, and it may be expressed as follows: Is there such a thing as absolutely right conduct, or are all standards of right and wrong relative, and dependent upon circumstances?

It is only comparatively recently that the older and traditional view has been challenged by the latter, and its principal proponent has been Joseph Fletcher in his book, *Situation Ethics*. He argues that what makes an act right or wrong is not some divine fiat or absolute standard, but whether or not in any situation it offends against the overriding principle of love. Given this premise, love may be used to justify any deed if the alternative course of action denies that love the chance to express itself.

Let us take some actual examples. Was Claus von Stauffenberg justified in attempting to assassinate Hitler in July 1944 if he honestly thought it would shorten the war? Was the woman who was a prisoner of the Russians at the end of the war justified in committing adultery because she knew that only if she was pregnant would she be allowed to return to her family in Germany? Would I be right in breaking into a man's house during his absence and stealing the revolver with which I had good reason to believe he was intending to commit a crime? Was Rahab right in telling the King of Jericho a whole string of lies to prevent his capturing the spies whom, for very good reasons, she had welcomed and concealed (Josh. 2)?

Now every Christian will readily admit that there are occasions on which he has to make a choice between the lesser of two evils, and not, as he would wish to do, between what is clearly right and wrong, between black and white. It is in fact a dilemma which faces us almost every day, often in trivial matters, when we have to choose between truth and politeness, and sometimes in those that are more serious. The Christian's argument is not that such situations never arise, or can always be avoided, but that the circumstances which may be held to justify a particular course of action do not of themselves make that action right. He insists that there is an absolute standard of right and wrong, of good and evil, but that in an imperfect world it is not always possible to apply that standard, and that sometimes therefore we have to choose the lesser of two evils.

Of course Christians believe that love is the summary of the Law (Rom. 13.10), because there is not one of the Ten Commandments which can be broken without in some way and to some degree offending the principle of love; but that is not the same as saying, as some do, that love is a substitute for the Law, and that if we love, then we can forget about the rules. 'Love God and do as you like' is a dangerous half truth.

Let us illustrate this from motoring. Every motorist knows that Care is the golden rule which should govern the behaviour of all road-users; but unless there are rules which define Care in terms which he can understand, he will not be able to apply the principle and exercise the care he should.

In the same way, unless there are rules which define the boundaries of love, we shall be left to interpret the word in the light of our own fallen nature, and are almost certain to get it wrong. It is true that in both cases once the rules have been learned and are engraved in our minds, then the principle will take over, like a sort of automatic pilot, and we shall find that we are keeping them without even thinking about them. That presumably is what the psalmist meant when he said, 'Yes, Thy law is within my heart' (Psa. 40.8). For him it was not just engraved on marble or written in a book, but stamped indelibly on his heart and mind.

If we may pursue the motoring analogy one stage further, we know that there are circumstances in which we feel justified, for example, in exceeding the speed limit, when we are trying to get someone to hospital, perhaps, or prevent a crime from being committed. But this does not invalidate the Highway Code, and we do not complain if we are convicted and fined, because we recognize the fact that it would be far worse for society if there were no rules at all than to have rules which in exceptional circumstances have to be broken, when it is felt that the alternative course of action might have even more damaging results.

While therefore there may be occasions on which the Christian and the 'situationalist' come to the same conclusion and act in the same way, their starting-points are quite different; and the Christian will approach any decision to do what he feels is not absolutely right with the utmost caution.

To begin with he will want to satisfy himself that there is no possible third course he could adopt. Could Hitler have been kidnapped, for example, or the police warned about the intended crime? Then he will need to think very carefully about the effect his action may have upon others to whom it will not be possible to explain the circumstances. I may think I have very good reasons for, so to speak, 'exceeding the speed limit', but what if others follow my example with disastrous results? None of us lives to himself (Rom. 14.7), and we have to be careful lest the liberty we feel it right to exercise in such matters become the cause of someone else's downfall (1 Cor. 8.9).

If I am finally satisfied that the only course open to me is the lesser of two evils, then I must not pretend to myself that it is good, and in taking it I must be prepared to ask for God's forgiveness. There is an interesting example of this in the story of Naaman. After he had been miraculously cured of his leprosy, he determined to go back to his own country to worship and serve the one true and living God. But he foresaw a problem. It was his duty to attend the King of Syria when he worshipped 'in the house of Rimmon', and this involved him in paying homage to a heathen god. Although he realized that it would now be wrong for him to do this, he knew also that it would cause great offence to the king if he did not. It was an awkward dilemma. Rightly or wrongly he decided that he should accompany the king on these occasions and continue the practice, but he was not entirely happy about it, and took the precaution of asking for forgiveness in advance (2 Kings 5.18).

The Christian's 'Highway Code' has always been the Ten Commandments (Ex. 20), but as amplified and developed by Christ Himself in the Sermon on the Mount. He said that He had come to 'fulfil the law' (Matt. 5.17), in the same sense that the outline of a map is filled in with rivers, mountains and towns, giving it a deeper content and a wider application.

Looking at the Ten Commandments as Christ looked at them, it is very hard to find any area of human conduct which cannot be brought within their framework. The first four commandments deal with man's vertical relationship with God, and tell us how He is to be honoured and served; and the last six are concerned with man's horizontal relationship with his fellow men – his parents and neighbours. They affect what we do (VI, VII, VIII), what we say (IX) and what we think (X); and they protect the four most precious things any of us possesses: our life (VI), our wife (or husband, as the case may be – VII), our property (VIII) and our reputation (IX).

It is clearly not possible, in the course of one short chapter, to deal fully and adequately with the subject of Christian behaviour, but there are four words which not only cover the Ten Commandments, but which also relate respectively, though not exclusively, to our professional, social, personal and spiritual lives. The four words are, Integrity, Charity, Purity and Humility.

Nothing distinguishes the Christian more sharply in his *professional* or business life than *integrity*. There is a oneness, a consistency about him, so that wherever you tap his life it rings true. Deeds are matched by words, and words by attitudes. He is a man of his word, who can always be trusted, and in whose hands other people's money, property and reputations are absolutely safe. In an age when pilfering has become an accepted way of life, when expense accounts are fiddled, and when people do not think twice about wasting their employer's time or using his telephone for private purposes, he 'walks uprightly' (Psa. 15.2): like David who, surveying the bribery and corruption in the midst of which he lived, but was able to affirm his own clear intention: 'I will walk in my integrity' (Psa. 26.11).

If integrity is the principal hall-mark of a Christian's professional life, then *charity* distinguishes his *social* life. It begins at home, as the commandment reminds us, with the respect and love he shows to his parents, and later on to his children (Eph. 6.4); for Christian charity is able to bridge the age-gap which we hear so much about today. Towards his friends he is generous with his time, his advice, and perhaps even his money; while those who for some reason oppose him have at least to admit that his judgements are fair, and that he treats them without rancour or bitterness; for he is always ready to believe the best. For him 1 Corinthians 13 is not just a place that he visits from time to time, when the mood takes him, like a sort of holiday cottage; it is his permanent home. He has learned to 'walk in love' (Eph. 5.2).

The mark of the Christian's inner, *personal* life is *purity*. For him this means very much more than refraining from things like adultery and fornication. It is a certain positive quality of life in whose soil evil thoughts of any kind simply refuse to grow and flourish. We are told that holiness is that without which we cannot expect to see God (Heb. 12.14); and conversely, if we may take a certain liberty with Proverbs 22.11, it means that 'he who loves purity of heart . . . will have the king as his friend.'

And in his *spiritual* life, in his relationship with God, the distinctive feature is *humility*. The word has had what might be called 'a bad press'. It is sometimes dismissed as a negative, defensive quality, reminiscent of the obsequiousness of Uriah Heap. But it is not like that at all. It is not self-depreciation, but self-forgetfulness. It is not pretending you are very bad, but forgetting you are very good. Humility is the ability to measure ourselves as God measures us, and to assess our strengths and weaknesses as they appear to Him. This means that we shall not shrink from responsibility as Moses tended to do (Ex. 4.1–17), nor exercise it in an arrogant and high-handed way as others have done, like Rehoboam (1 Kings 12.1–14). We shall not feel slighted if we are passed over for some post for which another is preferred; and we shall do big things without conceit, and little ones without complaint. This is what Micah meant when he said that the sort of person in whom the Lord delights is one who has learned to 'walk humbly with his God' (Mic. 6.8).

These fundamental virtues constitute the four walls within which Christian morality is built, and together they embrace not only the Ten Commandments, with the fuller teaching that Jesus gave, but practically all that we find in the Bible on the subject of behaviour. But of course it is in the life of Jesus Himself that we see them most vividly portrayed.

Not only did Jesus speak the truth, He claimed to be the truth, the very personification of it (John 14.6). He was the magnetic north by whose life people could steer with perfect confidence, because there was no inconsistency, and every trace of hypocrisy and unreality shrivelled up in His presence.

His charity was unique. Constantly we read that He 'had compassion' on people – the hungry crowd, the blind man, the demoniac at Gadara. His friends were the people He was able to help, the tax-collectors, the collaborators and sinners – not those whose pride and self-righteousness put them beyond the reach of His compassion and care. He was always at people's disposal, always ready to help, and however tired or busy, we never read that He refused the call of anyone who was in need. His patience was inexhaustible.

Now look at His purity. It is interesting how people were unable to attach any form of sin to Him. His question, 'Which of you convinces me of sin?' (John 8.46) left His critics speechless, and went unanswered all His life. There was nothing that people could accuse Him of, for although He liked to be known as 'the friend of sinners' (Matt. 11.19), there was never any suggestion that some of that sin rubbed off on to Him. People realized that He was 'holy, harmless, undefiled, separate from sinners' (Heb. 7.26) and completely without sin Himself (Heb. 4.15).

Finally, there was His humility. He might have come into this world as an angel, but He chose to be 'made a little lower than the angels for the suffering of death' (Heb. 2.9), and so He came as a man. He might have lived as a prince, served and honoured by His fellow men; but He chose instead the life of an ordinary working man, the village carpenter. He might have died as a hero, at the head of a great army of liberation against the occupying Roman power; but instead of that, 'He became obedient unto death, even the death on a cross' (Phil. 2.5–8). He, the Son of God, the Prince of Glory, the King of Kings, came as a man, lived as a servant, and died as a criminal.

We have seen what these qualities are, and we have studied them in the original, but how are they to be reproduced in us? How may we ordinary Christians show in our lives something of this Christ-like behaviour? The most obvious answer is 'by imitation'. Christ provides the perfect example, and we must try to copy it in our own lives. One of the most famous of all religious books has been written on this theme, Thomas à Kempis' 'Imitation of Christ'.

But the trouble most Christians find is that it simply does

not work. Have we not all had the experience of watching some great sportsman, or listening to a famous pianist, and then coming home and trying to reproduce what we have seen or heard? What has happened? We have fallen hopelessly, ludicrously short. 'It is no good,' we say, as we throw the golf club down or shut the piano in despair, 'I can't do it. It isn't in me.' We are quite right, and that is the nub of the whole problem. 'It isn't in us,' and we can't produce what isn't there.

But it is precisely here that Christ meets us and comes to our aid. His answer to our problem is not imitation, but inhabitation. In other words, His Holy Spirit, living within the Christian believer, is able to form in us the likeness of Christ. We become reproductions of the original picture, recordings of the original orchestra; and this is what C. S. Lewis means when he describes us as 'little Christs', 'models' or 'replicas'.

We touched upon this earlier, when we thought that the virtues of the Christian life are not like artificial flowers, or the goodies attached to a Christmas tree, but they are grown from within, like the fruit of a pear tree. The Christian is not asked to struggle vainly towards the standard which God has set, but he is empowered to reach it by the indwelling presence of the Holy Spirit. That is the basic difference between the Old Testament and the New, between life under the Law and life under Grace.

> Run then and work, the Law commands,
> But gives you neither feet nor hands;
> 'Tis better news the gospel brings,
> It bids you fly, and gives you wings.

This was what Paul meant when he said, 'The law of the spirit of life in Christ Jesus has made me free from the law of sin and death' (Rom. 8.2). If you throw a cricket ball into the air, you expect it to come down again at once under the influence of gravity; but if you throw a sparrow into the air, you expect it to soar away, because the law of life within it is superior to the law of gravity.

Of course, we must not expect this refining process to be quick or easy. We can be sure that the Devil will do all in his power to frustrate the purpose of God in trying to reproduce within us the likeness of His Son. One of the Devil's favourite devices is to try to develop a caricature of what God is trying to produce within us. If he cannot make us dishonest then he will try to make us almost neurotically scrupulous. If he cannot make us uncharitable, then we must be on our guard against his efforts to make us over-indulgent, soft and permissive. In the same way, prudery is purity which has been allowed to grow sour or rancid; and humility can degenerate into servility.

It is God's purpose, through the work of His Holy Spirit, to restore in us the image that was so badly spoiled, but never completely obliterated at the Fall: the image of His Son, Jesus Christ; and it must be the Christian's ambition that when the Lord Jesus appears 'we shall be like Him; for we shall see Him as He is; and everyone who has this hope purifies himself, even as He is pure' (1 John 3.2). An old Indian gold-refiner was once asked how he knew when the gold was completely refined. 'When I can see my face in it,' was his reply.

Speaking in Tunbridge Wells in 1942, shortly before his death, William Temple said, 'If I had to choose between preaching the gospel and social concern, I would have to choose preaching the gospel'; but he went on to say that happily he did not have to make that choice, because it was not a question of 'either . . . or . . . ', but 'both . . . and . . . '

When we refer this question to the Scriptures, it is clear from many parts of the Old Testament that social concern played a very big part in the thinking and the preaching of the old Hebrew prophets. Men like Hosea and Amos had a great deal to say about the corruption and injustice of their day. What was the good of a religion if it could contentedly co-exist with exploitation and greed on the one hand and with poverty and deprivation on the other? 'Take away from me the noise of your songs; to the melody of your harps I will not listen. But let justice roll down like waters, and righteousness like an everflowing stream' (Amos 5.23, 24). Social justice and national righteousness were a constantly recurring theme of the prophets, and a religion which did not work itself out along these two levels was unacceptable to God.

When we turn from the Old Testament to the New, the emphasis seems to change. The approach is personal rather than national; and the accent on love and charity rather than on justice, and on relief rather than remedy. The reason for this is that the prophets in the Old Testament and the apostles in the New were appealing to two quite different classes of people. Hosea and Amos were addressing the leaders of their country, the men of power and influence who, because Israel was at least nominally a theocracy, were often the religious leaders as well. These men were in positions of authority. They could remedy the system as well as relieve the suffering.

But quite a different situation faced the apostles. The Christian church did not take root in its earliest days among

the rich, the noble and the powerful (1 Cor. 1.26), but
among the working classes and the slaves. Its leaders therefore were in no position to influence the framing of policy.
Church and state were quite unrelated, and the apostles saw
their first social duty as relieving suffering, particularly
among their fellow Christians, and their responsibility in this
matter may be summed up in words which Paul wrote to
the Galatians: 'Do good to all men, especially to those who
are of the household of faith' (Gal. 6.10). For them charity
began at home.

We see the importance which the apostles attached to this
work, not in their undertaking it themselves, but in the
appointment of specially qualified men whom they called
'Deacons' ('servants' or 'waiters') to be responsible for its
administration and execution, leaving them free to concen-
trate upon the work for which they had been equipped and
ordained, namely the preaching of the gospel.

It is worth noting the qualifications which the apostles
required in this first generation of deacons (Acts 6.3). They
were in no sense 'second class Christians', chosen because
they were not good preachers or speakers; and it is interesting that the longest sermon recorded in the New Testament
was preached by one of their number – Stephen (Acts 7).
Far from it, for they were to be men renowned for their good
reputation, their spirituality and their wisdom. It is also
worth noting that this sort of social work is still regarded,
at least by the Church of England, as an important part of
the duty of the newly ordained deacon; for in the Ordinal
he is told that 'it is his office, where provision is made, to
seek for the sick, poor and impotent people of the parish . . .
that . . . they may be relieved with the alms of the
parishioners and others.'

In the light of all this, how are we to interpret and understand the role of the Christian church today? Is its duty to
relieve suffering or to remedy the system? Is the key word
'charity' or 'justice'? What responsibility has it for social
concern?

Surely it must be both. The Christian must take every
opportunity that comes to him as an individual, or to his
church as a community, of helping those in need (Jas. 1.27).
This will not interfere with his preaching the gospel, but
rather the reverse; for he will quickly discover that his

credibility as a preacher will depend upon his concern for
the welfare of the people he is trying to reach; and a man
who is hungry, cold or ill-clad is in no mood to listen to the
gospel.

But even in circumstances which permit no chance to
preach the gospel, the Christian will still want to do all in
his power to relieve suffering. There were probably many
people whom Jesus healed and helped and yet who never
responded to His teaching or became His disciples. Indeed,
the purpose of His healing ministry was not just to make
recruits, but to relieve suffering – 'because it was there'; and
in fact He told us Himself that whenever we come to the aid
of those who are in any sort of need we are in effect ministering to Him (Matt. 25.31–46).

But is that as far as we can go? Is relief work enough?
What about remedying the system? What about the Old
Testament injunctions of Amos, Hosea and others? So far as
this country goes, we are obviously not a theocracy in the
same sense as Israel in the eighth century before Christ; but
on the other hand we are in a far stronger position than the
Christian church was in the first century AD. Church and
state may not be synonymous, but at least the church has a
very powerful influence upon the state, and can affect its
legislation and policy-making.

This brings us to the vexed question of Christians and
politics, for there is a continual argument as to what role
if any the church should play in this respect. There are those
who say that it has no business to interfere, and others who
argue that there is no area of human life from which the
church with its message can rightly be excluded. The argument generates more heat than light, partly because people
never seem to be clear in their minds what they mean by 'the
church' or by 'politics'.

If they mean that the clergy should not enter parliament
(which they are not allowed to do anyway if they are in
the Church of England) then no one would quarrel with
them. The clergy are ordained to do a different job. But if
they mean that Christians should never have any say in the
way they think we ought to be governed, then of course they
are talking nonsense. If organizations like the Confederation
of British Industries, the Trades Union Congress and other
institutions can express their opinions and urge upon the

government certain lines of conduct, then why should not the Christian church be allowed to do the same?

Granted this right, it would seem that there are three special responsibilities which belong to the Christian church in this regard. First, it must preach 'national righteousness', just as the prophets did of old. Although the principal reason for doing so is that God has commanded men to be righteous, it is interesting how often righteousness and prosperity are linked together in the Bible, as cause and effect. Perhaps it is not surprising when we remember that righteousness and 'the fear of the Lord' so often breed those very qualities which make for individual and national prosperity: things like integrity, thrift, industry, self-discipline and generosity.

No one today, in this country, would make the mistake of equating the church with the working classes, as was the case in the days of the apostles. In fact it is often blamed for being too middle-class. It is unfortunately true that it does not in the main reach the vast mass of working-class people. The dockers of Southampton, the miners of South Wales and the car workers of the Midlands seem to find very little to which they can relate in the life of the church.

This is sadly so, but we must remember that there is a sense in which the Christian Faith tends to make those who embrace it become 'middle-class', because it develops within them those virtues which make for an improved standard of living. There is nothing new or magical about this. When the Bible says that 'the righteous shall flourish like the palm tree: he shall grow like a cedar of Lebanon' (Psa. 92.12), it is not suggesting some sort of reward, but simply stating a case of natural cause and effect. Perhaps very few of us would be able to echo from our own experience what David was able to write: 'I have been young, and now am old; yet have I never seen the righteous forsaken, nor his children begging bread' (Psa. 37.25), but there is no doubt that Christians do tend to rise in the world socially.

What the righteous does with his new-found prosperity or with the means he may have to achieve it, is another matter. David Sheppard in his book, *Built as a City*, deplores the tendency of the newly converted Christian to leave the deprived area where he first came into faith, and seek better conditions for himself and his family. And Sheila Cassidy, in the story of her life, *Audacity to believe* pays a great tribute to the 'worker-priests' who become slum-dwellers in Santiago, and describes her own feeling of guilt as she contrasts their manner of life with her own, as a Christian doctor living in a more residential area.

We are entering a sensitive and subjective area of personal life. Should a private soldier accept a commission if he feels that by doing so he will be depriving his fellow soldiers of the more direct Christian influence he can bring to bear upon them? Should the woman with great teaching and pastoral gifts accept a responsible administrative post in a big comprehensive school? How far the individual Christian should be influenced by the natural and healthy desire to 'get on', to improve his lot and realize his ambitions must be a matter for his conscience and perhaps the advice of his friends; though he must remember that they will sometimes want to justify their own ambitions by encouraging his.

But we have digressed from the point. We are concerned with national righteousness. But what is true on the individual level is also true on the national. If we could eliminate shop-lifting, tax evasion and smuggling – to name but three practices which stain our national life today – we could cut the cost of living and raise its standard overnight. A few years ago it was reckoned that what was stolen from the shops each year was equal to the annual agricultural subsidy. Shopkeepers have to cover their losses by putting up their prices, and so the innocent suffer for the guilty.

So much for integrity, and now what about thrift? One of the first things a young Christian is taught is the disciplined use of money, and the duty and privilege of putting some of it aside which can actually be given away to charitable concerns. Most people living in the affluent west can do without some of the expensive things they allow themselves, the costly hobbies, or holidays perhaps which they enjoy; for all too easily we allow the luxuries of yesterday to become the necessities of today. This is what many Christians try to do, and if there were more Christians, it follows that there would be very much more money available for those in need.

And when to honesty and thrift we add things like industry and hard work – a fair day's work for a fair day's pay – we can see at once how a country like our own has within its own hands the remedy for many of its problems, and the secret of its own prosperity.

To pursue this Utopian ideal a little further, imagine what would be saved on the prison services, the security guards and the police force! We are told that during the revival in Wales at the beginning of the century, the police in some places found themselves almost redundant, and had time to join some of the religious bands and choirs. And if this spiritual epidemic spread to other countries, so that we could beat our tanks into tractors and our guns into lorries (Isa. 2.4), we would find ourselves living in a world of unimaginable prosperity of the kind pictured for us in his poetical vision by the prophet Isaiah (Isa. 11).

This may all seem rather far-fetched and fanciful, and sad to say it probably is; but it does illustrate how inescapable is the equation between righteousness and prosperity, and it does serve to underline the fact that the problems in this country, and indeed throughout the world, are not primarily economic or political, but moral and spiritual. Let Scripture have the last word on the subject: 'Righteousness exalts a nation; but sin is a reproach to any people' (Prov. 14.34).

If the Christian's first duty is to preach righteousness, then his second responsibility is to consider whether he himself, or others whom he may be able to encourage and who are suitably qualified, can play any part in the social services, local government, parliament or in any other of those institutions which are closely concerned with the running of the country. In his book on 19th Century evangelism. *The call to seriousness'*, Ian Bradley draws attention to the astonishing number of committed Christians there were in parliament in the first half of that century; and it is doubtless largely to their influence that some of the great social reforms of that period can be attributed.

In the third place it is the Christian's duty to argue and even agitate for the sort of reforms and remedies he feels to be in line with the will of God. How far he should take part in petitions, protests and demonstrations will depend upon how he sees the stewardship of his time and the demand of his other commitments. He will not lose sight of his spiritual responsibilities, and he will remember that in these days there are many very good causes which are supported not only by Christians, but by men and women of other religions and of no religion at all, by humanists and agnostics, and which may sometimes safely and wisely be left to them to

champion. But at the same time, there have been occasions
when public opinion, mobilized by Christians, has served,
either locally or nationally, to prevent some mischievous
course of action, or to promote one that is right and good.

But we need to remember that however desirable it may
seem to change or to remedy the system, people, Christians
as well as others, simply because they are fallible human
beings, will never agree as to exactly how it should be done;
and there are many political, social and economic issues
about which it is impossible to say that there is a specifically
Christian answer. Perfectly sincere men and women,
earnestly wanting the best for their country as a whole, will
often differ quite sharply about the means of achieving that
very desirable end. Zeal must therefore be tempered by
tolerance, and, when no fundamental principle is involved,
by a willingness to compromise.

This is one reason why it would be undesirable if not
impossible to try to form a 'Christian' political party. There
are too many issues on which even Christians would fail to
agree. Who, for example, is able to say with any sort of
conviction whether monetary control or import control is
the more Christian way of running the country's economy?
It is far better in present circumstances that Christian breezes
should influence every party, so that politicians honestly
begin to seek, not what they want, but what they come to
feel is the will of God.

And we must also remember that politicians, like the rest
of us, are human, and that self-interest, or the instinct for
political survival, will very often dictate their decisions.
What hope, for example, would a political party have of
being returned at the polls if a plank in its electoral platform
was the promise (or threat) of a tax of even 1p in the pound
on all incomes over £5,000 which would be used directly for
the help of refugees or for assistance to the third world? It
would be committing political suicide. Such a clause could
only appear in its election manifesto if it was known that
there had been a nationwide revival of true religion, and
that the majority of the electorate were sincere and committed Christians: and then it would be unnecessary.

And so it has to be admitted that we only get the sort of
system that we deserve. That is why William Temple, if he
had been obliged to do so, would have preached the gospel

of personal redemption rather than the gospel of social reform; because in the last resort, you will only get the second when you have got the first.

13   The Problem of Evil

No one can be a Christian for any length of time without having to face the question, 'How can you believe in a God of love, when there is so much misery and suffering in the world?' For the atheist, of course, there is no problem whatever. There is no reason why a universe which has come into existence as the result of blind chance should be good rather than evil. The problem only begins if you believe, as Christians do, in a God who has the ultimate welfare of His creatures at heart.

Part of the problem is pretty straightforward, for a vast amount of human suffering is the direct or indirect result of man's sin; and unless we are prepared for God to turn us into robots, incapable of doing anything except at His dictation, we cannot fairly blame Him for the mess that we have made of the world.

The Marxist argues that what men call evil will disappear when we have established a classless society, and there is no more poverty or other environmental handicaps. But this surely is nonsense, for it takes no account of the fact that sin is not the preserve of the poor and deprived, but that the rich and prosperous are just as prone to evil-doing. You do not change the habits of a pig by keeping it in a drawing-room; and it is from the heart of man, and not from his environment, that there proceed things like pride, lust, greed, envy and malice (Mark 7.17–23).

The psychiatrist, on the other hand, would like us to believe that evil is the result of a thwarted libido, a sense of inferiority, or some form of 'personality defect', perhaps inherited. But if they are right, not only would we expect to see great moral improvements in those whom they treat, but also that they themselves would be noticeably better people than those who get along without their psychological expertise. But it is not so, and as Professor Joad says, 'as an explanation of the common-or-garden wickedness of ordinary man, of his pride, his unscrupulousness, his temper and his cruelty, it is hopelessly inadequate.'

Even if Christianity were not, as Christians claim it to be, a supernaturally revealed religion, and a purely human invention, it provides by far the best reason to account for the sinfulness of man; for it teaches that he was born with an innate tendency or bias towards evil, and that he can do no good thing without the help of God; and it traces the origin of this condition back to the mystery of the Fall. It is because of this event that men are by nature wicked. I use the word 'mystery', because of course there are little more than faint hints in the Bible as to the origin of evil itself, and we are left to suppose, as we have already seen, that in some pre-cosmic state there was a rebellion against God, and that the principal adversary, Satan, established a kingdom of darkness into which, at the time of the Fall, he successfully recruited man.

It is not difficult either to realize that there must be occasions when suffering comes to us as some form of punishment from God. It is a well-known fact that there are certain diseases which are directly attributable to sins of self-indulgence. The Bible is full of examples of the way God visited communities (Amos 1 and 2) and individuals (Prov. 3.11, 12) with His judgement upon sin; and the psalmist tells us that it was some form of affliction which turned him back again into the path of obedience to God (Psa. 119.67).

There is another form of suffering which is directly connected with human sin, and does not in one sense constitute a problem, and that is the persecution meted out to Christians by those who are dedicated to destroying their faith. The warnings which Jesus gave concerning this are too numerous to quote (John 15.20), and it is clear from many parts of the Bible that 'all who desire to live a godly life in Christ Jesus will be persecuted' (2 Tim. 3.12). Such persecution which has continued all down the ages, and is still practised and experienced today in many parts of the world, is perhaps inevitable when we remember that 'light has come into the world, and men love darkness rather than light' (John 3.19).

The Christian's attitude to this sort of suffering should be to rejoice (1 Pet. 4.12, 13), not for some masochistic reason, but because it is a way in which we can share in the sufferings of Christ (Phil. 3.10). It must not be supposed that this refers to the vicarious and sacrificial sufferings of Christ, but rather to the suffering which He still endures as one who is 'despised and rejected' by the vast majority of people. We are, so to speak, joining Him in His exile.

We can only imagine the sorrow and suffering which God must experience as He surveys this runaway world. Studdert Kennedy touches upon this theme in a very moving poem called 'The Suffering God'. He distinguishes between the sacrificial suffering on the cross, and the daily, eternal agony He must endure 'at all the vile deeds men do beneath the sun.'

> Then it must mean, not only that Thy sorrow
>   Smote Thee that once upon the lonely hill,
> But that today, tonight and on the morrow,
>   Still it will come, O gallant God, to Thee.

It was this same thought that made Henry Drummond declare on one occasion, after counselling some students, 'Oh, I am sick with the sins of these men. How can God bear it?' And it was what made Paul weep as he thought about those who had declared war upon Christ (Phil. 3.18).

It would not be so bad if we could share the optimism which prevailed at the turn of the century, and which was so rudely shattered by World War I. This was based upon the belief that man would move steadily upwards 'working out the beast, and let the ape and tiger die'. Lecturing on Decadence Lord Balfour struck a popular note when he said, 'There are, so far, no symptoms of pause or regression in the onward movement which for more than a thousand years has been characteristic of our civilization.' That lecture was delivered in 1908. He had only six years to wait before the dream he shared with so many was crumbled into dust. And it was a dream shared by many Christians, infecting some of our hymn writers, as we can still see.

> Nation with nation, land with land
> Unarmed shall live as comrades free;
> In every heart and brain shall throb
> The pulse of one fraternity.

How hollow such words sound today, three quarters of a

century later! It was a kinsman of Lord Balfour's, Lord David Cecil, who went much nearer the mark when thirty years later he said, 'The jargon of the philosophy of progress taught us to think that the savage and primitive state of man is behind us; we still talk of the present "return to barbarism". But barbarism is not behind us, it is beneath us'; and he goes on to observe, 'Christianity has compelled the mind of man, not because it is the most cheering view of human existence, but because it is the truest to the facts.'

So far then, whatever we may think about the suffering caused by sin, it doesn't present the real problem. Indeed, there is a certain grim logic about it. Man is given free-will but instead of using it to serve and please His maker, it becomes an instrument of rebellion and disobedience; and because his happiness depends upon a harmonious relationship with God, his disobedience brings misery to himself, sorrow to God and suffering to his fellow creatures. Cause and consequence are inevitably linked.

What constitutes the real problem of evil is those forms of suffering which cannot be obviously related to sin. There is the sort of person of whom Jesus said, 'Neither this man sinned nor his parents, that he was born blind' (John 9.3). What are we to say about those countless millions of innocent sufferers? Sinners they may be, but they are no worse than others, and why should they be singled out as the victims of some loathsome disease, a grim massacre, or be crushed to death when a tower block collapses upon them? (Luke 13.1–5).

We must remember that there is a sense in which the whole of creation has become involved and is infected by the downfall of man. Paul describes nature groaning, as though in the pains of child-birth, and waiting for the day in which it can share in the release of God's children (Rom. 8.19–21). It seems unavoidable, therefore, and has become part of the 'law of nature', that the innocent have to suffer with the guilty; for because of the solidarity and integral nature of God's creation, the effect of sin cannot be contained.

We are still living, so to speak, under the 'fall out' of man's original disobedience. Nature itself has been dislocated and rendered 'hostile' to God, and this hostility is seen in its capricious behaviour, in earthquakes, volcanoes, in the predatory habits of animals, in human disease, and

9

ultimately in decay and death. But for man's disobedience
we can assume that nature would be in perfect harmony with
its creator, and that none of these things would happen.

Now we are told that Jesus 'came that He might destroy
the works of the devil' (1 John 3.8), and 'that through death
He might destroy him that had the power of death, that is,
the devil; and deliver them who through fear of death were
all their lifetime subjects to bondage' (Heb. 2.14, 25). On
the cross Jesus destroyed, or at least mortally wounded, the
devil himself, while during His life He demonstrated His
power over the devil's works. Nature responded to His command. The storm was stilled. 'The shame-faced water saw
its God and blushed'. Sickness was healed, and finally death
itself was conquered. But this display of His power was not
meant to be the final establishment of His kingdom. That is
still future. Satan is still 'the prince of this world' (John
14.30). What happened was a demonstration, a pre-view,
an overture of that time when the kingdoms of this world are
finally subdued to His sovereign power.

It is for this reason that the Christian is an optimist; for
as he looks upon the suffering and sighing of men and
women, he draws hope and comfort from those apocalyptic
pictures which we are given in the Bible of that land of pure
delight which lies beyond the horizon which men call death:
that place where 'God shall wipe away all tears from our
eyes; and there shall be no more death, neither sorrow, nor
crying, neither shall there be any more pain: for the former
things are passed away . . . Behold, I make all things new'
(Rev. 21.4, 5).

Of course it is only too easy to parody this belief in a
world where evil will be redressed as 'pie in the sky when
you die'; and perhaps it has been used in the past as an
excuse for not trying to improve man's lot here on earth.
But it formed an integral part of the teaching of Jesus, and it
would be difficult to believe in a God who will not find some
way of compensating those who have lived down here with
the appalling handicap of heredity disease, brain damage or
physical deformity; or who have laboured under the grind-
ing disadvantage of orphanhood or cruelty, malnutrition or
manic depression. It is true that Paul was probably thinking
of those who suffered for their faith, but I think we may
fairly extend the application of his words when he said, 'I

consider that the sufferings of this present time are not worth comparing with the glory that is to be revealed to us' (Rom. 8.18).

It is easy enough for those who have never really suffered to wax eloquent and philosophize on the subject, and it is one which must be approached with great sensitivity; for it is a very traumatic experience when God seems to 'put forth His hand and touch' us physically, mentally or materially (Job 2.4). But I have rarely if ever met a Christian who has been embittered or soured by suffering and affliction. Again and again one goes to comfort someone, and returns humbled, encouraged and stimulated by the faith of a character which seems to have been enriched spiritually by the very things that are impoverishing it physically. From a body half paralysed or ravaged by cancer there has shone out a radiance of spirit, almost as though the person concerned had already caught a glimpse of 'that immortal sea'.

This is one reason why I cannot accept the view that all suffering is to be deplored, and that it is God's will that every disease should be cured, and that the only really spiritual exit from this life is through natural decay and senility. There are I know remarkable instances of seemingly miraculous cures which have followed the laying-on of hands, and there is good Scriptural authority for this ministry (Jas. 5.14, 15); but it does not seem to me that there is any for supposing that it is always God's will to heal the sick in this way, nor that those who continue to suffer should feel that for some reason they have forfeited God's pleasure and do not deserve such a cure.

And have we any right to single out one result of the Fall, namely human sickness, and argue that this alone should be abolished for all Christians everywhere? Why not storms, floods and other natural disasters which bring misery and loss to so many? Why not premature death, genetic deformity or pain of every kind? Why not the predatory habits of animals? Surely the answer is that 'we see not yet all things put under Christ'. We are firmly taught that the day will come when there shall be no more of these things, but if it is still future, have we any right to expect it to be part of our present and universal experience?

All the best commentators seem to agree that the 'thorn in the flesh' (2 Cor. 12.7–9) from which Paul prayed so earnestly to be delivered was some form of physical affliction – epilepsy, perhaps, or some kind of ophthalmic disorder. It seems to have been something from which normal and healthy people recoiled in disgust (Gal. 4.14), because he applauds the Galatians that 'though my condition was a trial to you, you did not treat me with loathing or contempt' (literally, 'you did not vomit'). It was clearly some sort of ailment or condition which was a constant source of embarrassment to him and to all who came into contact with him. Surely, therefore, if it were God's purpose always to restore people to full health, He would have done so in the case of Paul. The fact that He did not do so must mean that He has a purpose in allowing some of His servants to suffer, and we must now try to see what that purpose is.

First of all, as C. S. Lewis has said, pain and suffering can be 'God's megaphone' – the way in which He makes Himself heard above the noise and clatter of our over-busy lives. Many a Christian has found that an illness can be a blessing in disguise, as we saw in the case of David (Psa. 119.67). Perhaps the still small voice has not been able to make itself heard, and it has needed the megaphone to oblige us to rethink the structure of our lives, to learn new lessons in prayer, or to get some vital reading done. Joni Eareckson, a quadriplegic ever since a swimming accident at the age of seventeen, tells us in her story that learning some of the lessons that God has had for her behind her suffering 'has made all the difference in the world'.

One obvious lesson is that God can use sickness to teach us a greater dependence upon Himself. This may have been why He refused Paul's request for a complete recovery. So often we are tempted to think that God uses us because of our gifts, but very often He has to use us in spite of them. It may have been tempting for Paul to rely too heavily on his superb intellect, or his Hebrew upbringing as a strict Pharisee, or his Roman citizenship, or perhaps his exceptional conversion and revelations. His affliction reminded him that the treasure entrusted to him was in an earthen vessel (2 Cor. 4.7), that only weakness can receive strength and emptiness fullness. The megaphone was not wasted on Paul.

It is Joni Eareckson again who develops in her book another less frequently recognized reason why God allows 'bearing' to be the only form of 'doing' for some of His children. If a Christian can actually trust God and praise Him in the midst of suffering and affliction, does it not suggest that He, God, must be a very marvellous Person? If the attitude of the Christian towards his disability invites the question, not 'Why ever should God allow this to happen to you?' but rather, 'Who is this wonderful God you have got that you can still love and trust Him so, when He has done this to you?' Does this not glorify God in a unique way?

This was the place that Job reached, and no book goes more deeply into the subject of undeserved suffering than this one. Job endured every imaginable affliction – the loss of property, family and health. With the help of his friends (who were often more of a hindrance) he explored every possible explanation of what had happened to him. He rejected outright the simplistic ones, and though he could not fathom the profound ones, nothing would shake his faith in the final sovereignty of God. Bewildered, dazed, tempted and tried to the very limit of his endurance, he could still say, 'Though He slay me, yet will I trust in Him' (Job 13.15). Our natural reaction is to say, 'What marvellous faith!' But surely it should be, 'What a marvellous God who can command such faith!'

Another, perhaps more speculative line of thought, has commended itself to many. It is this: Are not some of the most noble virtues of which man, with God's help, is capable only seen and appreciated against the sombre background of suffering and pain? Even war, it is argued, produces comradeship, heroism and self-sacrifice on a scale seen at no other time; and we are bound to ask whether sympathy, compassion, courage and generosity could flourish or even survive in a world in which they had no opportunity to express themselves, and where there was no sorrow, no sickness, poverty or pain.

It is easy to caricature this line of reasoning, and to suggest that God allows some to suffer so that others may be kind to them; and taken in isolation, perhaps the argument will not stand up. But seen as part of God's overall strategy, which must include an eternal as well as a temporal dimension, it contributes a not insubstantial share of sense to our understanding of this problem. We are really back where we found ourselves in an earlier chapter – *O felix culpa* ...

But on this subject of all subjects it is terribly easy, as Job found, 'to darken counsel by words without knowledge' (Job 38.2). His own reflections and those of his friends ranged from deep philosophical insights to practical worldly wisdom; but when all is said and done, the only answer to this most inscrutable of all mysteries lies for us where it lay for Job, in silent submission to the sovereignty of God.

Our reaction to any personal tragedy or disaster often seems to go through three stages. The first is incredulity that this thing can possibly have happened to us. 'Not me, Lord!' we say in amazement. This is often followed by a period of resistance, even rebellion. 'Why me, Lord?' we ask in tones of resentment. But God wants to get us to the point of acceptance, when in tones of humble submission and trust we are prepared to say, 'Yes, me Lord.'

Amy Carmichael, herself a great sufferer, explores these attitudes in her own heart. There is no rest to be found in forgetting, in endeavour or aloofness, but only in acceptance.

> He said, 'I will accept the breaking sorrow
>   Which God tomorrow
>   Will to His son explain'.
> Then did the turmoil deep within him cease.
>   Not vain the word, not vain.
> For in acceptance lieth peace.

14   Life After Death

Death has been described as 'the last thing we talk about'. People make nervous jokes about it, but it is seldom a subject for serious conversation. Try raising it as a topic for discussion at a dinner party, and watch how the talk shrivels away into an embarrassed silence. People prefer to have it swept under the carpet.

But it was not always so. A hundred years ago things were different. In those days sex was the subject no one talked about, but death figured so prominently in everyone's thinking that it was unavoidable, and it was a subject which artists and novelists handled with confident if sentimental assurance.

The reason is not far to seek. A hundred years ago death was a far more every day experience than it is today. In large Victorian families there were nearly always one or two children who failed to survive infancy, while others were carried off in early life by one of the many infectious diseases now so happily eliminated. In Haworth Parish Church you can see a plaque commemorating the entire Brontë family, every single member of whom pre-deceased and was buried by the father.

Today, in spite of the hazards of modern travel, there are many fewer things which people can die of. Cancer in this country accounts for about 20 per cent of all deaths, and cardiac disorders for a number more; but the average expectation of life of the population has doubled in the last hundred years or so, and thought and discussion about death may be conveniently pushed over the horizon, and postponed until middle age and beyond.

But there is another reason for the present unpopularity of the subject, and it concerns the faith and hope which our forefathers had in a life beyond the grave – a faith and hope which are much less widely and confidently held today. Because of this the Victorians were far less embarrassed by the subject than we are, and less afraid to discuss it rationally.

It was a most popular subject for their hymns and poems, and if we accuse them of eulogizing it with epitaphs like 'Called Home', or 'Called to High Service', then we, with some of our modern expressions tend to demean and trivialize it.

What then is the Christian view of the life to come? Are the dead raised up? And if so, what form will their existence take? It was to answer these two questions that Paul wrote his famous fifteenth chapter of First Corinthians. The first was a Jewish question; for although belief in some sort of immortality had become part of orthodox Jewish faith, there were still many, notably the Sadducees, who scoffed at any kind of resurrection (Matt. 22.23). It is interesting that neither in this chapter nor elsewhere does Paul make any reference to the occult, or to any psychical or para-normal phenomena, but bases his belief purely and simply upon the resurrection of Christ. 'Since our message is that Christ has been raised from death, how can some of you say that the dead will not be raised to life?' (1 Cor. 15.12).

He then goes on to deal with the specifically Greek objection (1 Cor. 15.35). 'How can the dead be raised to life? What kind of body will they have?' In answering this question he will have nothing to do with the old idea, so popular with the Greeks, of mere immortality of the soul. In this view the soul of man is released at death, like a bird from a cage, to spend eternity, one must assume, as a disembodied spirit floating about in a kind of mystified coma. Nor does he, and nor does Scripture anywhere else, entertain the notion, so popular in some eastern religions and enjoying a certain revival today, of some form of reincarnation, whereby our exact place in the batting order in the second innings will be determined by our performance in the first: the outcast eventually returning as a Brahmin (if he has accumulated enough merit or *karma*) and vice versa. Equally abhorrent to Scripture is any suggestion that we lose our identity in some sort of 'world soul' – 'a pulse in the eternal mind' – like a drop of rain falling into a puddle, or a blackberry losing itself in a pot of bramble jelly.

What the Bible does teach on this subject is something very much more concrete and definite. It teaches us that God has prepared another body for us – a 'spiritual body'

(1 Cor. 15.44) which will be adapted to an altogether different kind of existence: as different from our present earthly existence as that of the butterfly from the caterpillar that preceded it.

Perhaps we get some clue as to the nature of this resurrection body when we think of Jesus Christ's. In His case it was the same, and yet different. He was recognized, but seldom immediately. He was capable of all the normal functions, and yet not subject to natural laws. His body was physical, and yet incorruptible and immortal.

It would perhaps be unwise to build too firm a doctrine on the parable of Dives and Lazarus (Luke 16.19–31), but we can safely say that it teaches us two things which will distinguish human beings beyond the grave. First, they will retain their individuality and identity as recognizable persons; and secondly it appears that heaven and hell will be irremediably separated with 'a great gulf fixed' between the two which, while it may not deprive the one of the knowledge of what is going on in the other, will make any form of physical communication between the two impossible.

It seems clear, therefore, from what has been said so far, that the resurrection is something which applies to everyone, good and bad. 'Resurrection' itself is a neutral experience. The important thing is whether it is 'the resurrection of life' or 'the resurrection of damnation' (John 5.29).

This must now lead us on to a discussion of heaven and hell. What do Christians believe about this subject? First of all, the Bible always speaks of them as places – 'up there' or 'down there'. They are never just states of mind, but geographical locations. It does not follow from this that if we could travel far enough we would find them somewhere in outer space, but they are places which, if they have not yet been prepared for us (John 14.2), God will be able to bring into existence in a moment of time, just as He did before, and just when the time is ripe and it pleases Him to do so (2 Pet. 3.10–13; Rev. 21.1–5; Isa. 65.17, 66.22).

But is there no middle ground? No 'intermediate state' of any sort? There is no doubt that from very early days Christians did believe in a form of 'purgatory', where the believer (if you could call him that) was prepared, disciplined and refined for the final vision of God. But it must be admitted that this belief, although attracting many supporters, rested upon the flimsiest scriptural evidence. In fact almost the only passage that can be adduced in its defence was that in which Christ spoke of certain sins which would not be forgiven 'in this life or in that to come' (Matt. 12.32).

This doctrine was roundly attacked at the Reformation as an heretical accretion. It was argued that souls could be freed from sin by Christ alone, without their own good deeds, and therefore if saved in this way went straight to heaven. This is not to say that there will be no room for growth or progress in heaven, or that all men and women will be given equal responsibility; but simply that so far as our qualification to enter is concerned, our destiny is decided while we are still here on earth.

But what are we to understand by 'hell'? There are three words which the Authorized Version translates into this English word 'hell': *Sheol, Hades* and *Gehenna. Sheol* is derived from the Hebrew word meaning 'valley' or 'hollow', and later came to be associated with the 'deep' of the sea. It is simply the place to which the dead descend when they die. It has mournful rather than penal associations, except in so far as all death is the consequence of human sin, and premature committal to *Sheol* was sometimes regarded as a special form of punishment (Psa. 55.15).

Hades was the Greek word representing the realm of the dead – literally, 'the place of shades or shadows'. It was the word used in the Septuagint to translate *Sheol*, and it is intended to convey the same idea – the place of the departed. It is worth noting that Paul, in quoting Hosea 13.14 in 1 Corinthians 15.55 substitutes the word 'death' (*thanatos*) for *hades*.

The word *Gehenna* literally meant 'the valley of Hinnom', (Josh. 15.8, 18.16) and was situated outside the city of, Jerusalem, where children had been sacrificed by fire to Molech (2 Chron. 28.3, 33.6); though there is nothing to indicate exactly who Hinnom was. It was foreshadowed by Jeremiah as 'the valley of slaughter', and therefore became a natural symbol for the divinely appointed place of punishment (Mark 9.44–48).

There can be no doubt that the New Testament and Jesus Himself depict hell (*Gehenna*) as a place of eternal misery and regret. Even if we are not meant to take literally the idea of the 'fire' and the 'worms' (Mark 9.43–45), Jesus would hardly have used such metaphors if they had exaggerated the true state of affairs.

The uncompromising teaching of Scripture on this subject has led Christians to try to think of some less unpalatable alternative. There are those, for example, who believe in what is called 'conditional immortality', that is to say, the total annihilation of the wicked and the survival of the good.

Immortality, according to this view, is not a necessary attribute of the human soul, but conditional upon his faith and conduct while in the body on earth. Historically this idea has received very little support from theologians, and it was almost unknown and certainly condemned until the last century; it rests upon a very fragile exegesis of certain parts of the New Testament. It may be comforting to think of unbelievers as non-existent rather than as living in permanent exile from the presence of God, but such a view depends upon an interpretation of Scripture which has never enjoyed wide acceptance.

The other view is known as 'universalism,' the belief that a loving God will find a way back to Himself, even for those who have disobeyed His gospel and rejected His Son. Some notable scholars, such as Origen, have flirted with this idea, but it was strongly attacked by Augustine, and has never found general favour, because if anything there is less support for it in Scripture than there is for annihilationism. Moreover, can we really suppose that Christ would have suffered the sharpness of death and the judgement of His Father upon sin if all the time He knew that even those who had rejected what He had done for them would be pardoned? And what are we to make of His command to preach the gospel to everyone (Mark 16.15), if in the last resort it does not matter whether they believe or not?

It seems therefore that in neither direction is there a retreat open for us from the stark reality of the New Testament teaching on this subject, namely that man's eternal destiny is settled in this life according to his response to the claims of Christ. The fact that we can see no way of reconciling eternal retribution with the character of an all-loving and all-powerful God must not be allowed to disturb our

faith that there is an answer, even if it is beyond our limited
human minds to grasp. We ought by now to be used to such
'irreconcilables' or paradoxes. That which exists between
God's pre-destination and our own freewill is another; and
indeed, they are only to be expected when we are dealing
with mysteries beyond our understanding. Such equal and
opposite truths are like the two wires leading to an electric
light. If you have only one, you are left in the dark. If you
try to join them together and find a logical answer, you
cause great confusion. Your only hope is to treat them as
equally true and equally important, but to keep them apart.
They are like parallel lines; they only meet in infinity.

But what about the heathen who have had no opportunity
to hear the gospel, or the mentally handicapped or little
children who have had no chance to understand it? Are they
too, because they have not responded to what they have
never known, to be swept into everlasting darkness?

Scripture is very silent on this subject, perhaps because an
important incentive for preaching the gospel would disappear if we knew that those who were deprived of the
chance to hear it were no worse off. There is in English law
what is known as 'an extra-statutory concession', the right
of the executive in certain exceptional cases to waive the
strict application of the law; and there are hints in the Bible
that God will exercise His sovereign right to act in this way
(Matt. 19.14; Rom. 2.14–16), and that we may safely rely
upon the Judge of all the earth to do what is right (Gen.
18.25).

In some ways the Bible teaching on the subject of heaven
is easier to follow, for it is clear from the very earliest days
that the Israelites thought of heaven as the dwelling-place
of God, and could pray, 'Look down from Thy holy habitation, from heaven' (Deut. 26.15) ; and Jesus Himself taught
us to pray, 'Our Father who art in heaven' (Matt. 5.45).

But the Bible does not picture God as dwelling there in
splendid isolation, for we read of 'the host of heaven' who
worship Him there (Neh. 9.6), and Jesus spoke of 'the angels
who are in heaven' (Mark 13.32) ; while Christians too are
confidently encouraged to look forward to 'an inheritance
. . . reserved in heaven for them' (1 Pet. 1.4). Heaven therefore may be thought of as the present abode of God and His
angels, which will also become the final destination and

home of His saints.

When we begin to study the nature of heaven more closely, we are obliged to take refuge in symbols, for this is the only way open to us to describe what is so infinitely beyond our experience and our ability to understand; 'for eye has not seen, nor ear heard, neither have entered into the heart of man, the things which God has prepared for those who love Him' (1 Cor. 2.9). Symbols also serve another purpose, for they often act as a kind of shorthand (£, @, +, &c) and save a long and sometimes difficult explanation.

And it is in this way, using a sort of symbolic shorthand, that John describes the Revelation he has received, in the last book of the Bible. He wrote it while living in exile on the island of Patmos in the Aegean. He is thought to have been there from AD 81–96, when under the Emperor Nerva he returned to Ephesus. A grotto is still shown to tourists, where he is thought to have received his vision.

And so, in highly figurative language we are given a glimpse of what heaven will be like; and we find amongst other things that there will be no sea there, no sun and no sin. The Israelites did not like the *sea* (Rev. 21.1). For them the river was the symbol of peace and tranquillity (Isa. 48.18; 66.12), while 'the troubled sea', incapable of rest, reminded them of the spiritual turmoil of the wicked (Isa. 57.20). To them too the sea spoke of separation and division, and its final disappearance suggested a place where severed friendships would be reunited, and where partings and farewells would be no more.

And then we are told that the city will have 'no need of the *sun*' (Rev. 21.23), 'for the glory of God will lighten it, and the Lamb is the light thereof.' I take this to mean that all those things which have brought us pleasure and happiness here on earth, all the light we have enjoyed from nature, art, literature, friendship and love – all the bright lights – will be swallowed up in the glorious presence of God. How brightly these things have shone in this dark world! But we shall not need them when the day breaks and the day star arises (2 Pet. 1.19); 'for with Thee is the fountain of life; and in Thy light shall we see light' (Psa. 36.9).

No sea and no sun! Two of the things which perhaps we

relish as much as anything else on earth! But it is God's way
of telling us that He has prepared for us 'such good things
as pass man's understanding', and that we shall not even
miss those things which have given us so much pleasure and
enjoyment on this earth.

> O how the city of our God is fair
>   If without sea, and sunless though it be,
> For joy of the majestic beauty there
>   Men neither miss the sun nor mourn the sea!

And finally, there will be no *sin*. Just as sin was excluded
from the garden at the very beginning (Gen. 3.24), so now
we are told that 'there shall in no wise enter into the city
any thing that defileth, neither whatsoever worketh abomination or maketh a lie' (Rev. 21.27). If heaven is where God
is, then it is also where Satan is not. The Prince of Darkness
will be finally and for ever overthrown, and all his angels
with him. He is pictured as being 'cast into the lake of fire'
(Rev. 20.10), and it would hardly be possible to imagine a
more vividly terrifying or complete form of destruction: to
be burned and drowned at the same time.

And so it is at this point that the victory won by Christ
upon the cross all those years ago will finally be celebrated.
At last we shall see all things put under Him (Heb. 2.8),
and every knee bowed before Him (Phil. 2.10); He will be
all and in all (Col. 3.11) on that day when 'the kingdoms
of this world are become the kingdoms of our Lord and of
His Christ; and He shall reign for ever and ever' (Rev.
11.15).

Created to Praise

Derek Prime

'If we begin by praising God in our prayers, there is little doubt that we shall end up as we ought. We shall both pray correctly and end by praising Him all the more. To this end we were created.'

Derek Prime's comprehensive guide to praise is detailed, lively and biblical. He shows praise to be man's chief end, considers the themes of praise in the Bible, and explains its place in song, prayer, trials, everyday life, death and heaven.

For all who want to develop this essential Christian activity, *Created to Praise* is indispensable.

New International Version Holy Bible

The finest modern translation

More and more people are discovering the
pre-eminence of the New International Version.
John Stott and I Howard Marshall are among the
Christian leaders who recognise its importance.
The Gideons and the Navigators are among the
organisations who are enthusiastically adopting it.
Scripture Union produced identical booklets
featuring the NIV and the RSV: the NIV is
outselling the alternative by eight to one. For
accuracy, for readability it is the Bible for today . . .
and tomorrow.

*'Of all the modern translations I have read, I have
found none better than the New International Version.
It is superb!* – John Blanchard